how to survive in leadersh
Catholic Sch

A personal reflection for headteachers and deputies

CONTENTS

DEDICATION

For Janet and the boys

+

*In Memory of Francis Gabriel Friel (1930-2010)
who lovingly passed on the tradition*

FOREWORD

To be a good Catholic school headteacher means to do theology on your feet, to walk the God talk. This book clearly describes both the demands and the rewards of this journey, as Raymond Friel reflects on his many years of experience as a school leader. At the heart of the book lies his conviction that everybody involved in Catholic education should have the opportunity to enter more deeply into their vocation. Parents and teachers are called by God to a special role in forming young people; the headteacher has to enable them to realise this in practice. Students need help to hear the call of Christ in their lives and the headteacher must make the school a place that enables that call to be discerned amidst the cacophony of other voices that beset young people. Above all, heads themselves need to be sustained in their vocation. Their vocation includes not only their leadership of this part of the Church's mission, but also their own life of prayer and their personal relationships. No job can be a vocation; if it were, redundancy and unemployment would mean that somebody had lost not only their job but also their vocation. Work is one part of a vocation that begins with baptism and the Christian life that flows from that. It then finds expression not only in work but also in life as a married or single person, as an ordained or consecrated person. Each person's vocation is unique because it brings together these diverse elements into one special life. Leaders in Catholic schools need to keep hold of their own vocation, in all its different parts, helping their students discover that they too are called to a unique combination of love and work derived from their life as children of God. St Paul asked people to "lead a life worthy of the calling to which you have been called" (Ephesians 4:1) and this book issues the same invitation to Catholic school leaders.

Fr Christopher Jamison OSB
Director, National Office for Vocation
Catholic Bishops' Conference of England and Wales

INTRODUCTION

I'm a serving Catholic headteacher and this book has been written primarily for other Catholic headteachers, those aspiring towards Catholic headship, members of senior leadership teams, and the governing bodies of Catholic schools. I've been a Catholic headteacher in secondary schools for twelve years and I hope that some of my reflections and experiences may help those who are on a similar journey, although every headship is unique, just as every Catholic school community is the same but different. I am grateful for this opportunity to share my own experience and understanding with fellow professionals.

In the course of my research I visited sixteen schools and interviewed the headteachers and groups of their students. In the limited amount of research into Catholic education I have come across I found very little engagement with our primary schools. I therefore decided that seven of my school visits should be to primary schools, with the rest being secondary and one a sixth form college. I also interviewed three former headteachers who are still working in Catholic education in senior roles.

I chose the schools to visit either because I knew them or because I had heard about them. I did not make a deliberate attempt to find a range of schools according to Ofsted grades, although the schools I visited ranged from "outstanding" to "requires improvement". The schools were mostly maintained or academies, with three being independent. Given my time constraints I could not venture too far from

my home base, but I did manage to cover four different dioceses in the South West, the London area and the Midlands. I do not make any claims of academic rigour for this book. Professor Gerald Grace has set the bar high in that respect in *Catholic Schools: Missions, Markets and Morality*. I do however hope that the insights of my colleagues and my own experiences may offer some practical support and encouragement to all those who lead our Catholic schools or who are hopefully considering that option.

The other group who are almost entirely absent from academic research in our sector are governors, those committed volunteers who take on so much responsibility for the strategic direction of our schools. There is good support material for school governors nationally, but very little specifically for the governors of Catholic schools. I would encourage all those who have found this book to be of use to look out for its sibling by Sister Judith Russi, about how to survive in governance in a Catholic school.

Raymond Friel

CHAPTER 1

The Revolution of Tenderness – "The Joy of the Gospel" and Catholic Schools

Pope Francis has called upon the faithful to light a fire. The Church has a long interest in such activity, going right back to the time of Jesus. In Luke's Gospel, we find the haunting story of the encounter between two disheartened disciples and a stranger on the road, which ends with dying embers being fanned into a flame. They are on their way out of Jerusalem, the place of disaster, where all their hopes have ended with the public execution of their master. The stranger asks them what they are talking about on the road. In a moment of terrible irony, they chide him for being the only one who doesn't know about the things that have been happening in Jerusalem, without realising that he was at the traumatic centre of the drama.

But he wants them to share their pain with him, and asks the shortest question in the New Testament, the question *par excellence* of all those who accompany the broken and bedraggled on the road: "What things?" (Luke 24:19). They tell the stranger their story and how they had hoped for so much from their dead prophet. Jesus then chides them for being so "slow of heart" and gives the best seminar on salvation history ever heard by students of the Gospel. They press him to stay for supper and he vanishes from their sight at the breaking of the bread.

It is only then that they recognise him and say to each other: "Were not our hearts burning within us while he was talking to us on the road?" (Luke 24:32). Their slow, sorry hearts have been enflamed and they set out that same hour back to Jerusalem, glowing in the dark. No wonder John Shea, the American poet-theologian, described Jesus as the "arsonist of the heart".

In his first full publication, "The Joy of the Gospel" (Latin title: *Evangelii Gaudium*), Pope Francis exhorts the faithful to "light a fire in the heart of the world."[1] It is a call to renewal, a new summons to mission. Throughout the document there is the same loving impatience the stranger showed to the numbed disciples on the road – *why are you heading in the wrong direction with such heavy hearts?* Francis calls for new commitment and generosity on our part, but does not burden us by asking for some heroic individual undertaking. Inspired by a power much bigger than themselves, the disciples practically ran all the way back to Jerusalem. Any renewal in the energy of evangelisation is always the work of the Spirit. Our job is to step into the "great stream of joy"[2] and open ourselves to the Spirit who "inspires, provokes, guides and accompanies in a thousand ways."[3] This is a call to all Catholics in pastoral work, including the governors and headteachers of Catholic schools. We are part of the mission of the Church. We are being called back to the source to recover ourselves and to renew our creative engagement with the world:

whenever we make the effort to return to the source and to recover the original freshness of the Gospel, new avenues arise, new paths of creativity open up, with different forms of expression, more eloquent signs and words with new meaning for today's world.[4]

This is the challenge for school leaders. We are being called back to the Gospel, back to Jesus Christ, who never fails to resonate in the hearts of young people when his extraordinary message is presented to them with imagination. We are being called to a major exercise in mission renewal. We are being challenged to engage creatively with the Gospel so that our young people will hear the word in new and meaningful ways. If any part of the Church is well placed to lead this mission it is our schools, where the energy of the young is renewed every day and the energy of adults is nourished by this natural source. In this chapter I will try and provide some prompts inspired by Francis in the hope that we can generate a much bigger conversation about this *kairos* moment in the life of the Church.

The First Proclamation

Not everyone welcomes this Pope's "back to basics" fervour. There are many, including me, who struggle with his blunt invitation to live like a Christian with a missionary heart. He reminds us by his example that Christianity is a *lifestyle*, not a long list of beliefs to be

ticked off, or membership of an exclusive club, but a way to live in this world as a follower of the poor Jesus. I find myself looking in some discomfort at my nice car, and house, and suits, and wondering what's the difference between me and the hard-working headteacher round the corner who makes no claim to follow Jesus? Francis has well and truly bothered our conscience, much in the same way his patron St Francis of Assisi did many years ago. But the overwhelming view in the conversations I have had with headteachers is that this pope is exactly what we need:

He disarms us by everything he says and does. He models it, there's an integrity and authenticity about this guy which I find fascinating because he's saying "Look, I'm a sinner like the rest of you, pray for me." He says things about the Church and I think, "crikey!" Now whether we can actually take that on board layered down in terms of nationally and diocese, I don't know, but he's given the likes of me the courage to be far more outspoken about some of the things I feel quite strongly about.

Former Secondary Headteacher, still in Catholic education

What I've found really refreshing is that there seems to be a move away, slowly, from academia and a move towards real things and real people and real problems and concerns and worries that we're all dealing with, rather than writing a book or a pamphlet… That's what Jesus did. He walked the talk, talked the walk, and this move away from the policies and all of that to a bit of humility is a huge step forward.

Primary Headteacher

There is a new confidence in the air and a sense of permission to be bolder, more courageous. Francis acknowledges that the Church, like any community of human beings, is frail and will fall, but he says that, "the evils of our world – and those of the Church – must not be excuses for diminishing our commitment and our fervour."[5] We have been forced to confront the dark side of our Church in recent years (Francis is even stronger; he calls it "evil") and have been pained by the questions of our young people about what is going on. This should make us humble. It should also, in the mind of Francis, take us back to the core message, which is unchanged by the behaviour of those who dare to proclaim its richness. It leaves us wide open to claims of hypocrisy (one of the things which really riled Jesus) but it does not change the message:

Pastoral ministry in a missionary style is not obsessed with the disjointed transmission of a multitude of doctrines to be insistently imposed… the message has to concentrate on the essentials, on what is most beautiful, most grand, most appealing and at the same time most necessary.[6]

I do not believe that this message in any way lessens the importance of teaching the fullness of doctrine and the tradition in our schools. More urgently than ever, our young people need to grow in understanding of the knowledge of the faith because they are not hearing about it anywhere else. I think what Francis is saying is *please don't stop there and don't become obsessed with it at the expense of the essential message*. "The Joy of the Gospel" has something of the excitement of the apostolic preaching of the early Church. Francis uses the phrase "first proclamation" to sum up the heart of the message which our young people need to hear:

On the lips of the catechist the first proclamation must ring out over and over: "Jesus Christ loves you; he gave his life to save you; and now he is living at your side every day to enlighten, strengthen and free you".[7]

If you're looking to review your mission, it's not a bad place to start. We can no longer take for granted what our children and young people know already about Jesus and salvation, but we will know them well enough to adapt the message to their needs. Our primary role as educational leaders in the Church is to join the Bishop of Rome in the first proclamation of the Christian faith. What that ends up sounding like on a Monday morning in each of our schools is down to the sensitivity and skill of individual leaders. More importantly, what that *looks like* in each school will depend to a great extent on the integrity of the leaders.

PAUSE AND REFLECT

▲ How would you express the "essentials" of the Gospel message for your community?

▲ What "eloquent signs" will convey the original freshness of the Gospel?

▲ Will the "first proclamation" make sense to your students and staff? Do you need to find a new language for your context?

Sacred Grandeur

Charles Darwin, in the final sentence of his monumental work *On the Origin of Species*, concluded that, "there is grandeur in this view of life."[8] I'm not sure if the reference is deliberate, but there is an echo of Darwin's words when Francis calls us to a, "fraternal love capable of seeing the sacred grandeur of our neighbour, of finding God in every human being."[9] Francis does not have the same formidable intellectual reputation as some of his predecessors but he is a very well-read Jesuit and it would not surprise me if he was subtly bringing a Christian perspective to Darwin's great vision of evolution.

I am not a theologian (unless being a serving Catholic headteacher counts as being a practical theologian), but it seems to me that the theology of Francis finds its inspiration in Matthew's "Judgement of the Nations" (25:31-46). There we are faced with the radical proposition that a righteous life doesn't have much to do with observance or belief, but in looking after the lost and the least, since in doing that, "you did it to me," says God (Matthew 25:40). I remember

using that passage in my assembly at the beginning of the Year of Faith as part of a "back to basics" message for the students and telling them that it was all summed up in that remarkable story. I also remember that, as always, the students listened to me politely, but it was only when the Gospel message became a wonderfully expressive dance, followed by a cheeky two-minute film in which students were interviewed about how hard they tried to be nice to people every day, that the message hit the mark.

It seems to me that the theology of Francis is also the theology which underpins Vatican II, a theology which sees grace (the active presence of God) as part of human nature. There is a long tradition of another theological world view, known as the Augustinian view, which regarded human beings as hopelessly fallen. In this view, which many of us grew up with, only a strenuous spiritual training programme could bring us the reward of the grace of God. It led to a lot of guilt, of course, because who among us is capable of such spiritual athleticism? But that is not the theology of the most recent Council of the Church, it is not the theology of Francis, and it is not a theology which has any hope of inspiring the young. Vatican II talks about the "Godlike seed"[10] which has been sown in all people and is the reason for the dignity and destiny of every person. *That* is the kind of theology you could build a Catholic school on. If the "sacred grandeur" of our students and staff were a lived reality, and all our operational and strategic decisions flowed from that perception, we would be fulfilling our mission to the world.

It is not always easy in school, of course, to see the divine seed in everybody, every day. There are those days when you are doing the "hard yards" and having real trouble seeing any sacred grandeur in the Year 6 boy who has just thumped another student, or the Year 10 girl who has said something very cruel on Facebook about a vulnerable student, or the member of staff who is goading you with tetchy emails. It is even harder to see the sacred grandeur in individuals in episodes of history when evil holds sway in human hearts. We must never be glib about this and subscribe to a superficial optimism, just because we believe that grace is everywhere. *It is*, but the Church has always known that human beings are a mixed blessing and for every person who allows the Godlike seed to grow, there are others whose circumstances seem to provide no opportunity for that growth.

It becomes very hard to see the good, or God, in people who do great harm. But that is the limit of our seeing. It does not change the deeper truth that we are in fact dealing with a graced reality. And many people who struggle with that will be encouraged after reading "The Joy of the Gospel". There is a bracing quality to the writing of Pope Francis, a robust lack of self-pity, the world view of a man who has seen poverty and suffering but is still convinced that God dwells in all our brothers and sisters. He knows that in dealing with people there is risk, but the Christian is called to self-giving (*kenosis*) and if you've ever felt like hiding in your office from the angry parent or the querulous member of staff (and I assume most of us have) then put this on your wall and read it every day:

the Gospel tells us constantly to run the risk of a face-to-face encounter with others, with their physical presence which challenges us, with their pain and their pleas, with their joy… True faith in the incarnate Son of God is inseparable from self-giving, from membership in the community, from service, from reconciliation with others. The Son of God, by becoming flesh, summoned us to the revolution of tenderness.[11]

I have never felt called to be part of such a grand and noble project as a "revolution of tenderness". It is not new theology, it is certainly not radical. It is just expressed in Latin-American poetry we have not heard before. Francis takes us back to the Gospel where this revolution was given its finest expression in the life of Jesus. He reminds us that the secret is in the way Jesus looked at people: he did not see sinners, he did not judge them, he did not burden them with rules, he saw "beyond their weaknesses and failings"[12] and he loved spending time with them, even when he thought he was just about to have some quiet time for reflection with his friends (Luke 9:10-11). This is one of the many very practical challenges of headship, which will be covered in more detail in a later chapter; the problem of availability. It is easy to convince yourself that your day needs to be filled with important matters, and no doubt they are important, but the message of the Gospel, the message of Francis, is that there is nothing as important as face-to-face encounter with our brothers and sisters, with Jesus. In my research I met many headteachers who bore exemplary witness to the priority they gave to face-to-face encounter, often ministering to adults as much as children:

I've just been talking to a mum about domestic violence and I would say to you that I'm not sure how much a document would inform the way I dealt with that, rather than my own faith and experience.

Primary Headteacher

Francis calls us to a revolution of the heart, and young people are its vanguard. None of this is very far from the daily reality in our schools. I think that is why every headteacher I have spoken to has responded with such enthusiasm to Francis. He is speaking our language. However long it takes for the reforms Francis is calling for to take effect in the wider Church, our schools in the meantime are already there in terms of receptivity to this message. When our headteachers look at their children coming to school in the morning, they glimpse the grandeur Francis speaks about, bad days notwithstanding:

I think there's a goodness, I mean, we've just walked around the school seeing there is goodness in every single child and each morning when I come to work, when the kids stream in through the gates and I think, "Why am I here?" the children always elevate my sense of purpose when they smile at you…

Primary Headteacher

Francis exhorts us further, not just to see the sacred reality of our brothers and sisters, but to walk with them in their need:

The Church will have to initiate everyone – priests, religious and laity – into this "art of accompaniment" which teaches us to remove our sandals before the sacred ground of the other (cf Exodus 3:5).[13]

Everyone who works in a Catholic school, no matter what their role, is a student of the art of accompaniment. We are called to be *with* our young people throughout their years in our schools and the Road to Emmaus is our exemplary text. When that kind of thinking takes hold in a school it informs a whole set of decisions. Many schools use the language of "journey" and organise their staff and curriculum in the best way to support their young people while they are with them.

Throughout this book we will find many points of convergence between the expectations of the Church and the State for Catholic schools. From different starting points, the sacred and the secular mind (although the reality is never that dualistic) arrive at the same conclusion when it comes to safeguarding. The State has given increasing attention in recent years to promoting the dignity and well-being of the child, often prompted by egregious cases of harm (for example the death of Victoria Climbié in 2000 which led to the Laming Report in 2003 and the Every Child Matters framework). The Church has also been on a painful journey when it comes to learning how best to protect children and young people from the harm inflicted by some adults.

In April 2014, new statutory guidance on safeguarding was published for schools and colleges. *Keeping Children Safe in Education* (a much shorter document than its predecessor) defines safeguarding and promoting the welfare of children in quite functional language to do with protection from maltreatment and, "taking action to enable all children to have the best outcomes."[14] As we will see later on when we look more closely at the language used by Ofsted, the secular State needs to be as neutral as possible in its use of language. It no longer has any foundation or authority for using religious or spiritual language. But Catholic schools have no such constraints – in fact we should and do use the richness of our tradition to express our aims. Our commitment to safeguarding, which can be expressed in the introduction to all our policies, will include everything the State asks of us but our inspiration, our foundation, is the belief in the "sacred grandeur" of our children. That is why we are never content with mere compliance, but always strive for best practice.

PAUSE AND REFLECT

- ▲ Is the "sacred grandeur" of our children and staff evident in the policies and practices of our schools, especially with regards to safeguarding?

- ▲ Do we have as many opportunities for face-to-face encounters with our community as we should?

- ▲ As school leaders, how much of our day is spent with people and how much with paper?

Blessed are Those Who are Poor

Then we come to perhaps the very heart of the message of Francis, which is not unique or radical, it's just that we haven't heard it expressed so clearly or consistently for a while. Again, it is rooted in the Gospel and writ large in the documents of Vatican II. It resonates down the years from the very mouth of Jesus: "Blessed are you who are poor" (Luke 6:20). Matthew lets his community off the hook somewhat by saying: "Blessed are the poor *in spirit*" (Matthew 5:3) and that is often the preferred version of the Beatitudes. But in Luke there is no ambiguity – he is talking about the economically disadvantaged, the actual poor. From the very beginning of his pontificate, Francis has made this a central part of his preaching:

There can be no room for doubt or for explanations which weaken so clear a message. Today and always, "the poor are the privileged recipients of the Gospel"… We have to state, without mincing words, that there is an inseparable bond between our faith and the poor. May we never abandon them.[15]

There is also an inseparable bond between the poor and our schools. In this country, the education of the poor in Catholic schools was seen as a priority from the outset. Professor Gerald Grace's *Catholic Schools: Mission, Markets and Morality,* a seminal work on the mission of Catholic schools in England, provides a helpful overview of this history. He quotes from the first synod of the province of Westminster, following the restoration of the hierarchy in 1850: "The first necessity… is a sufficient provision of education adequate to the wants of our poor."[16] This imperative is stated again as a clear priority at Vatican II in the "Declaration on Christian Education", a foundational text for any Catholic headteachers or governors reviewing the mission of their school. In that document, as with Francis, there is no room for ambiguity about the priority:

The sacred Synod earnestly exhorts the pastors of the Church and all the faithful to spare no sacrifice in helping Catholic schools to become increasingly effective, especially in caring for the poor, for those who are without the help and affection of family and those who do not have the Faith.[17]

Francis exhorts us to consider not only the needs of the actual poor but also the "new forms of poverty and vulnerability", which he entreats us to draw near to, "even if this appears to bring us no tangible and immediate benefits."[18] This has a particular resonance for Catholic schools, when there is such pressure for every penny of "investment" to show tangible and measurable benefits, but again in this area there is a considerable convergence between the priorities of the Church and the priorities of the State.

In England and Wales since 2011 schools have received funding specifically to support disadvantaged or potentially vulnerable students. Headteachers have been held accountable for this "pupil premium", and Ofsted inspections are increasingly focused on the academic impact of the funding on the students supported by it: those who have been in receipt of free school meals at any point in the previous six years, Children who are Looked After, and children from Forces families. This approach has been broadly welcomed by Catholic schools, but the danger is that by focusing only on students supported by the "pupil premium", other vulnerable young people may lose out on support and our mission may be compromised.

I would argue that central to the mission of any Catholic school must be a sophisticated understanding of the "new forms of poverty and vulnerability" and a significant investment in supporting those students who fall into that category. We need to bring our best thinking to that exercise and ask ourselves if we know as much as we need to know about our students? A good practical exercise for any group of Catholic leaders would be to discuss what we mean by the "vulnerable". Have we included young carers, the August-born, those who have lost a parent, the sibling-bullied, as well as those with special educational needs or disability and those whom we are well trained to identify and support through our constant focus on child protection?

PAUSE AND REFLECT

- What is our understanding of the new poor and vulnerable in our school and the quality of support they receive?

- Does our focus on "pupil premium" compromise our commitment to all the vulnerable in our school?

- Does the headteacher take a personal interest in the most vulnerable children, those with special educational needs or disability, or who are in care?

The Common Good

Another major theme in "The Joy of the Gospel" which has relevance for Catholic schools is the affirmation of a principle which has a long and consistent presence in Catholic thinking: a commitment to the common good. Our schools have never been encouraged to see themselves as closed communities for the education of Catholic children only. We have always been invited to be "outward facing" and to consider ourselves as part of the mission of the Church which is to transform society and bring about the Reign of God. In *Christ at the Centre*, which contains a very helpful checklist of the characteristics of a Catholic school, Monsignor Marcus Stock reminds us that, "the common good consists of three elements: i) respect for the dignity of the human person; ii) social well-being and development; and iii) peace and justice (*Catechism of the Catholic Church*, 1905-1912)."[19] One of the main documents of Vatican II, "Pastoral Constitution on the Church in the Modern World" (Latin title: *Gaudium et Spes*), refers to the common good in Gospel terms which seem to foreshadow Francis when it says:

> … *everyone must consider his every neighbour without exception as another self, taking into account first of all his life and the means necessary to living it with dignity, so as not to imitate the rich man who had no concern for the poor man Lazarus.*[20]

Catholic social teaching, or the detailed working out of what the "common good" means, is sometimes called "our best-kept secret". But that is changing and, with the encouragement of Francis, the change will gather pace. In some dioceses, bishops have called for the social teaching of the Church to be integrated into the curriculum of Catholic schools from reception to Year Thirteen. In the past there has been some suspicion of this agenda. It is too political, too leftist, but if that is the case then Jesus was a card-carrying Communist. The Church may not always have preached the message strongly in every age, but it is clear in the Gospels that an essential element of the Reign of God is a critique of power and a commitment to the dignity of the person.

The way we have read the Parable of the Talents (Matthew 25:14-30) perhaps illustrates the point. In most of my Catholic schooling, the parable was used as a way to motivate us to make the most of our abilities. The single talent given to the third slave was his natural gift and he was "wicked and lazy" because he buried his gift. It didn't seem to occur to anyone that the master in this reading of the parable was an unlikely candidate for God. He does not contradict the slave when he is accused by him of being a "harsh man" making money through the exploitation of other people, or reaping where he had not sown. And does anyone recognise God in the portrait of a master who would take away from the most vulnerable the very little they have?

For a reading of this parable which makes much more sense and will better resonate with students, *The Parables of Jesus* by Fr Denis McBride is an excellent place to start. He points out that the talent received by the slave was *money*, about six thousand denarii; quite a lot of money. The point of the exercise was to raise more money with usurious loans. The third servant can therefore be seen as the hero of the parable since he breaks the cycle of exploitation and stands up to the harsh master. If the parables generally invite us to take a stand next to the character that best illustrates the Reign of God, where should we stand in this one? Fr McBride sets out an interpretation which makes more sense than a morality tale about not practising your piano scales:

Given Jesus' instruction to his disciples on the dangers of riches (e.g. Matthew 19:23-26), the abuse of authority (Matthew 19:25-28), and respect for the little ones (Matthew 18:1-7) the parable's interpretation as a coded critique of rich landowners' abuse of their economic power would seem more consistent with Jesus' own values. [21]

In his exhortation, Francis does not hesitate to speak truth to economic power, and like a true prophet he rails against the priorities of an age in which a drop in the markets is headline news but the death of a homeless man on the street passes unremarked. Nor does he allow us the comfort of sitting in the pews lambasting the current age for its wrongs. He keeps bringing it back to us and the type of behaviour in which we are fully implicated. The greatest danger he sees in today's world is the, "desolation and anguish born of a complacent yet covetous heart, the feverish pursuit of frivolous pleasures, and a blunted conscience." [22]

The Church has not always been able to speak with real authority about covetous behaviour when it was so clearly attached to its own considerable assets. The truth hidden in plain sight for much of history is

that the Church has been rich and has sided with the rich while preaching the Gospel of the poor Jesus. Francis caused world headlines when he refused to live in the papal palace and was content to be driven around in the back of a Ford Focus. This is the kind of Gospel example which sets hearts on fire.

In the critique of power and consumerism we have had much support over the years from our exemplary charitable groups, such as CAFOD. They have developed a sophisticated Gospel understanding of the use of resources in our world, a modern-day reading of the Parable of the Talents which, for those with ears to hear, makes us think twice about the cookie in our hand, or the shirt on our back. This is the kind of Church Francis wants. There is hardly any mention of sexual behaviour, which many of us heard a lot about in our Catholic upbringing. No one is saying that these things are not important or any Church teaching has changed, but the implication is we have had enough of all that for now. Go back to the Gospel. What do you find there? Teach that.

Our faith by its very nature seeks the good of others and we are called to inspire in our young people not only charity for the neighbour at our gates, but the courage to challenge the rich man who promotes and sustains an unjust system. In his typically direct style, Francis tells us that, "Christian preaching and life, then, are meant to have an impact on society." [23] And by society he means the family of the human race. The Church has always of course been universal, or trans-national in its outlook, but with such a long tradition of Euro-centric leadership, it could not make any real claims to be global in its culture or thinking. Now we have a Pope from the far corners of the earth, as he joked himself, who has been tested in a different cauldron, and brings a very different perspective. We have become accustomed to the cliché of the "global village", but with the rapid advance of digital networking and the global economy that is now very much a reality.

A global village needs global citizens, and I would argue that this concept should be central to the mission of Catholic schools in the twenty-first century. Francis is well aware of this when he says, "we need to pay attention to the global so as to avoid narrowness and banality. Yet we also need to look to the local, which keeps our feet on the ground."[24] Again with Francis there is a kind of street wisdom in his words and ideas, a common-sense view of the common good. We must be global but we must not get so carried away with the scale of that perspective that we forget the needs of our brothers and sisters around us. In England and Wales at the beginning of the twenty-first century, as Cardinal Nichols reminded us very strongly in media interviews just before he was made Cardinal, there are families living in conditions which deserve to be called a scandal. Or as one secondary headteacher, who serves an inner-city community, put it to me:

Children born into a very wealthy society, and we are a very rich country, go without breakfast, can't afford to go on a school trip, and can't afford a school uniform.

Secondary Headteacher

[1] Pope Francis, *Evangelii Gaudium* "The Joy of the Gospel", 271. Found at: **www.vatican.va**

[2] Ibid., 5.

[3] Ibid., 12.

[4] Ibid., 11.

[5] Ibid., 84.

[6] Ibid., 35.

[7] Ibid., 164.

[8] Charles Darwin, *On the Origin of Species* (London: Penguin Classics, 1968).

[9] *Evangelii Gaudium*, 92.

[10] Second Vatican Council, *Gaudium et Spes* "Pastoral Constitution on the Church in the Modern World", 3. Found at: **www.vatican.va**

[11] *Evangelii Gaudium*, 88.

[12] Ibid., 141.

[13] Ibid., 169.

[14] Department for Education, *Keeping Children Safe in Education* (Department for Education, April 2014). Found at: **www.gov.uk/ government/publications/ keeping-children-safe-in-education**

[15] *Evangelii Gaudium*, 48.

[16] G. Grace, *Catholic Schools: Mission, Markets and Morality* (Abingdon: Routledge Falmer, 2002), p. 8.

[17] Cited in Ibid., p. 18.

[18] *Evangelii Gaudium*, 210.

[19] M. Stock, *Christ at the Centre* (London: Catholic Truth Society, 2012), p. 9.

[20] *Gaudium et Spes*, 27.

[21] D. McBride, C.Ss.R., *The Parables of Jesus* (Chawton: Redemptorist Publications, 1999), p. 88.

[22] *Evangelii Gaudium*, 2.

[23] Ibid., 180.

[24] Ibid., 234.

CHAPTER 2

God's Dream — the Culture of Vocations in Catholic Schools

Next I would like to consider what a culture of serving the common good might look like in a Catholic school. How can we encourage our young people in this day and age to prepare for such a life when the prevailing culture often invites them to develop covetous hearts and to think solely in terms of material and physical advancement? Catholic schools have always had a counter-cultural dimension but in this respect we have our work cut out for us. It takes us back to a very basic question asked by the rich young men and women of our age – what is the secret of eternal life? Catholic school leaders often start here when they are reviewing their mission. What is the point of this life and what is the point of our education? What are we preparing our children and young people for and what is the best way to do that? Francis puts it this way: "If we wish to lead a dignified and fulfilling life, we have to reach out to others and seek their good."[1] He follows a long and consistent line in Catholic educational thinking, which is that we are preparing our young people not only for their ultimate end but for the good of society. So how can we prepare them for such lives at the beginning of the twenty-first century?

I think the answer to this question is tucked away in the long list of things which should define a Catholic school: building a culture of vocation. In my Catholic youth, vocation meant a calling to the priesthood or religious life, but that thinking has quite radically changed as we see in "New Vocations for a New Europe", sometimes just referred to by its Latin subtitle, *In Verbo Tuo*, the final document of the Congress on Vocations to the Priesthood and to Consecrated Life in Europe, which met in Rome between 5 and 10 May 1997. It was produced by a number of Vatican Congregations, including Catholic Education. Taken together with "The Joy of the Gospel", I think "New Vocations" is the key to unlocking a new wave of confident thinking in our schools, which will resonate with the best in secular thinking about what a great education should look like at the beginning of the twenty-first century.

The document begins with an overview of the spiritual and moral landscape in modern Europe. There is none of the scathing critique or sense of cosmic drama which has sometimes been a feature of the Church's engagement with the modern world. It is concerned above all with the breakdown of any sense of moral consensus:

Like ancient Rome, modern Europe seems similar to a pantheon or great temple in which all the "divinities" are present, or in which every "value" has its place and its niche.[2]

This is the age our young people are growing up in, the age of "pick and mix" spirituality, where the individual is king and queen and every truth is as good as the next. In our Catholic communities we have also seen the weakening of the social structures which have contributed so strongly to the religious formation of the young: the parish and the family. Among today's young Catholics, there is not the same adherence to the faith *in toto* which seemed to define previous generations. In 2009, the Catholic Youth Ministry Federation (CYMfed) published a fascinating piece of research, *Mapping the Terrain*,[3] which everyone who seeks to understand the mind of young Catholics should read. The research demonstrated the ability of young Catholics to hold what seem like contradictory views. It showed an alarming level of stress in young people, especially about exam performance, and concluded that many young Catholics have a strong sense of the spiritual but may not be able to articulate this in Christian terms. Eighty-three per cent of the respondents selected at least one word from the following cluster to describe the Church: authoritative, boring, cautious, conservative, established, exclusive, traditional. The voice of one young Catholic summed up the position of many:

I'm not a day-to-day Catholic, I'm sort of RC. I always break a couple of the old rules in the book

but I wouldn't go around saying I'm a Catholic but the views I have are Catholic definitely.

Male, 18, London

Dr Richard Wilkins, a Catholic headteacher in Brentwood, interviewed a sample of Catholic secondary headteachers in the course of his own research and asked for their perceptions of today's young people. In his discussions the headteachers observed a tendency among young Catholics, "to self-construct Catholic identity rather than conform to a definition of Catholic drawn by traditional authority. If the pupils in our schools describe themselves as Catholic, they are likely to do so on their own terms."[4] The reality is that this has probably always been the case more than has been recognised, but it is only very recently that young Catholics, or indeed adult Catholics, have been given the kind of voice we can hear in the CYMfed research. "New Vocations" goes on to consider the relationship of young people to the Church in language which seems to foreshadow the findings of the research:

Often, young people do not see in the Church the object of their search or the place where their questions are answered and their expectations fulfilled. God is not the problem, the Church is.[5]

It is such a painfully honest appraisal of a situation which many in Catholic education will recognise. Our young people mostly do not go to Church, that is undeniable, but to hear an official document say that it is the Church's problem, not theirs, is truly humbling and seems to foreshadow the brave approach of Francis.

The Cool Generation

The authors go on to describe the moral and spiritual situation of young people today. They express sadness at the number of young people who, "have no will to live, to believe in something, to work towards great ends, to hope in a world which can become better even thanks to their own efforts."[6] All of us who serve in Catholic education have an acute sense of the dangers and challenges facing our students. We could all bring to mind young people we know who are gripped by sadness, depression, or a lack of purpose. Some, as they get older, become possessed by the dark glamour of nihilism and fall into subcultures where they become difficult to reach. There is a view that the current generation of youth is the most self-absorbed and apathetic in human history, and it's a view that doesn't always come from the older generation.

A recent article on the BBC website's News Magazine featured the work of Adam Gray and Sam Fuchs, two twenty-nine-year-old digital artists and founders of the Hella More Funner collective in San Francisco. They spend hours searching the internet for images which they then use to create collages. Their views on their own generation are sobering. "Everyone's sort of mentally obese," says Fuchs, commenting on the digital lives of his peers. "I feel like distraction has a big part to do with our generation's story." There is a lot about relationships in their artwork but there is a post-modern weariness when they scan the bigger picture. "We will not be a great generation," says Gray, "we are too self-absorbed, spending most of our time on frivolous things, like photos of ourselves. We are cool kids, we are the cool generation."[7] Too cool to care?

Most headteachers will probably think of the inspiring words of Nelson Mandela during the Make Poverty History campaign when he said the opposite, and called on the current generation to be great. The words of the young Americans also find an echo in Pope Francis' description of the modern age as the "feverish pursuit of frivolous pleasures". The information overload of the digital culture, according to Francis, leads to, "remarkable superficiality in the area of moral discernment."[8] I'm sure the founders of Hella More Funner would agree with that assessment. Our young people are encouraged to live on the surface of themselves and to project their self-portraits, sometimes without any caution, into the digital sphere.

I know that many of us working in Catholic schools will only partly agree with the "Generation Cool" thesis, since we will know many young people who are passionate and committed and open to life. However, there will also be an unsettling recognition that there is truth in this view. I would argue that part of our role as Catholic educators is to provide a more compelling vision for our young people, to go back to the source and to find a narrative to inspire them. There is no point in reverting to the old script of moral outrage and condemnation of the modern world. The people are no longer listening: that message will fall on stony ground. We need to write a deeper and richer account of the person than that which is offered by the modern age. "New Vocations" provides us with some of the language and a framework for that script. It provides a vision of what we are called to in this life and exhorts educators to do all they can to develop a culture of vocation so that young people will grow up with reasons for living and hoping.

The Dream of God

The definition of vocation has changed in a generation. "New Vocations" makes it very clear that every person has a vocation, a purpose, connected to the simple act of existing:

The vocation is the providential thought of the Creator for each creature, it is his idea-plan, like a dream found in God's heart… Every creature expresses and is called to express a particular aspect of the thought of God. There he finds his name and his identity.[9]

It is beautiful poetry and what our young people need to hear: they are a dream found in God's heart. It is our great challenge to convey the message to them in ways which not only make sense but will seize their imagination and help to form them as young global citizens who will follow God's dream for them and feel themselves called to serve. If we are truly following God's plan for us then we will inevitably seek the good of others. Moreover, life will open up to horizons of wider possibility than what we can arrange for our own advancement.

The ability to dream and think big is also part of this vocational culture, that wonder that allows the appreciation of beauty and the choosing of it for its intrinsic worth, so that it might make life beautiful and true, that altruism which is not only an emergency solidarity, but which is born of the discovery of the dignity of every brother and sister.[10]

This summons to bigness of life (see also: magnanimity as a Christian virtue in the theology of Thomas Aquinas) has much the same dynamism as the writings of Francis. We see the same foundational theology and vision of the common good, the dignity of every brother and sister. We feel the same call to the "Big Gospel", as Richard Rohr calls it, the Gospel of life to the full, of dying to the small self, of life in the spacious freedom of God's overwhelming forgiveness. Let our schools not be filled with Generation Cool, but Generation *Called*, and let us see ourselves as the promoters of that call, helping young people to discover what their call is, depending on their gifts:

*True vocations promotion can be carried out only by those who are **convinced** that in every person, no one excluded, there is an original gift of God which waits to be discovered.*[11]

The emphasis on the word "convinced" is not mine, it is in the document. The authors convey their own passionate belief that when we look at our young people we should see giftedness and a calling to serve. In schools, especially in secondary schools, we have a duty to provide independent advice and guidance on *careers*, which no doubt we do well. But without compromising any aspect of what we are required to do, we can expand the remit to include the requirements of the Church for all people, so that the circle of the State's reasonable requirements sits within the bigger circle of the Church's vision.

The Element

The Church's belief in innate giftedness is shared by many thinkers who increasingly question our educational system and its fitness for purpose at the beginning of the twenty-first century. There is a wealth of literature on this subject and any overview is beyond the scope of this book, but I would like to mention one thinker, Sir Ken Robinson, whose work is very close in many respects to the Church's vision.

I first heard Ken Robinson at a conference before I read his work. I would recommend any busy headteacher to search for his TED lectures on the internet (Technology, Entertainment, Design: a global set of conferences owned by the private non-profit Sapling Foundation) as an excellent first encounter with this engaging Liverpudlian, who now strides the world like the proverbial intellectual colossus from his base in Los Angeles; except he doesn't really stride. At the SSAT conference where I first heard him, there was silence in the packed hall when this solitary figure limped on to the stage and stood in the spotlight. Childhood polio had left its mark on his body and seemed almost the foundational drive for his belief that every child has to discover their "element", their "original gift" when so much of our educational system seems designed to drain the creative energy out of them.

Many headteachers I know will take issue with Robinson's argument, but for me there's a great deal of evidence to back up his argument. The Catholic headteachers I have met have the same instinct as Robinson for seeing the child as unique and for seeking out the best in them. The point is always better illustrated from real life rather than in the abstract, like the headteacher who told me:

We have a particular child with a statement of special educational needs who won't even achieve a Level 2 in Year 6 but she's by far the best altar server that we've ever seen, so there's an opportunity for her to shine and I think as a Catholic school it's looking at the person rather than the outcomes.
Primary Headteacher

Robinson's main thesis, "that we are all born with tremendous natural capacities and that we lose touch with many of them as we spend more time in the world,"[12] is very close to the thinking of "New Vocations". The starting points are very different but the end point looks similar. The sources of inspiration for Robinson range widely across cultures and throughout history. "New Vocations" returns to the Gospel for its source of inspiration and considers, like Francis, how Jesus encountered people in his ministry. His human engagements were an opportunity to confront the person, "with the strategic question: 'What will I do with my life?', 'What is my path?'"[13] We see him again and again setting people on the way to life – "Your faith has saved you; go in peace" (Luke 7:50). "New Vocations" outlines five "pedagogical attitudes" which are developed within the Gospel, following the example of Jesus and the way he calls people to life. These five attitudes are well worth the consideration of Catholic school leaders and could provide us with a framework for a genuine culture of vocation:

To Sow

The exemplary text for this attitude is the Parable of the Sower (Matthew 13:3-9). Christian vocation is a dialogue between God and the human person, we should remember that. We are only sowing seeds, or rather we are only nurturing the seeds sown by God. A key to vocations development is nurturing the seeds at the right time. When in the young person's journey do we start to ask them questions about their "original gift" and what they might be called to do with it? It is skilled work and must be sensitive to the age of the person. When I was ten, like most of

my generation, I wanted to be an astronaut, closely followed by playing football for Scotland and scoring the winning goal in the final minute of the World Cup final (a day dream which has proved embarrassingly persistent). And yet, "not asking the question at the right time could prevent the sprouting of the seed."[14]

Do we make time in our schools for these conversations to take place, or does the pressure of the curriculum squeeze out any opportunity for encounter? I did have a wonderful moment in my school recently when we were interviewing for a teaching post. The candidate in front of me was a former student at our school. I asked her why she was attracted to the post and she said that in Year Seven her form tutor said to her, "You'd be a great teacher." That "seed", that comment, stayed with her, and ten years later she was sitting in front of me in her "element", bringing her "original gift" back home. She got the job.

> PAUSE AND REFLECT
>
> How and when do we nurture the seeds of giftedness and calling in our young people?

To Accompany

The Road to Emmaus, which is where we started, is the exemplary text for this attitude. The two disciples are seen as the image of so many young people today, "a little saddened and betrayed, who seem to have lost the desire to look for their vocation."[15] In many ways a lot of their prophets have been taken away from them. In my youth, the main institutions of public life, including the Church, still had moral authority and its representatives were accorded respect. Consider how that has changed in a few generations and how many of the estates have fallen in the public's estimation: the Church (abuse scandals), the City (the financial crash), Parliament (the expenses scandal), Fleet Street (phone hacking). As one of my colleagues said, our young people have no "elders" to guide and accompany them. It seems that all we are left with is a culture of vacuous celebrity (and even that has come under a very searching spotlight with some high-profile abuse cases in recent years). While walking one day on a beach in Scotland I came across these words scraped in the sand: "Where are the heroes?" Good assembly material, I thought, as I took the photograph and then later had a moment of genuine sadness as I imagined a young poet asking her question to the empty sky.

Part of our culture of vocation must be to create heroes for our young people. My generation grew up on the lives of the saints. If those stories are well told, they should grip any generation. The other exemplary text used to illustrate this attitude is the beautiful story of encounter when Jesus meets the woman at Jacob's Well in John's Gospel, a vocational conversation which also shows God's liberty in seeking his messengers everywhere and in everyone. The teachers are not always who we think they are. This woman, clearly an outcast collecting water at noon on her own, is turned around by Jesus and becomes a missionary to her own community. In a telling detail, she leaves her jar behind as she runs back to tell her community all about this prophet, glowing at midday.

The authors of "New Vocations" use the image of the well to represent the sources of meaning our young people are searching for in the complexity of today's world:

To accompany a young person means knowing how to identify the "wells" of today; all of those places and moments, those provocations and expectations, where, sooner or later, all young people must pass with their empty jars, with their unspoken questions, with their deep-seated desire for authenticity and the future.[16]

It is a beautiful metaphor: when our children come to us with their empty jars, what do we offer them? When we opened a chaplaincy provision for our new sixth form, we called it "The Well".

PAUSE AND REFLECT

Where are the "wells" in our schools, in our partnerships, in our dioceses?

To Educate

After sowing the seeds of future possibility, helping them to discover their giftedness on the journey of accompaniment, it is a question of educating the young person. Here, "educating" means drawing out (*e-ducere*) from him or her what they have in their heart, even what they do not know, especially about themselves. On the road, Jesus knows what they are thinking but still asks the question – "What things?" – so that they can open themselves to him and verbalise their sadness. Every day in school these conversations will be taking place in the nooks and crannies of our buildings. It requires skilled and careful work, and a listening heart.

There is a quotation, which I think is wrongly attributed to the poet Yeats, that education is not about filling a pail, but about starting a fire. We will consider the different types of education at greater length in a later chapter, but for now it is enough to say that for Catholic schools education must be about more than transmitting knowledge. A more convincing version of the famous quotation comes from the classical author Plutarch who says that "The mind is not a vessel to be filled, but a fire to be kindled."[17] In Catholic schools, education is about blowing into the soul's embers, creating the conditions where the young can flourish, listening to what is in their hearts and helping them to discover what they are going to offer the world.

PAUSE AND REFLECT

- ▲ How well do we listen to our young people in school?

- ▲ Do we inspire them with possibilities?

To Form

Formation is the culmination of the pedagogical process outlined in "New Vocations". The young person is offered a way of being in which he or she recognises his or her identity. This has surfaced in various ways in Church thinking in recent decades: the identity of the human being in the modern age without God. Pope Francis puts it this way:

Some people think they are free if they can avoid God; they fail to see that they remain existentially orphaned, helpless, homeless. They cease being pilgrims and become drifters, flitting around themselves and never getting anywhere.[18]

This is beautifully said, but I wonder if it would make any sense to your students or your staff? We have a real challenge here to convince the young people of today, and even the good people who work in our schools, that they are "helpless" without God. The reality is that for most people, who are relatively well off, well educated, and have more opportunities for stimulating leisure than ever before – it really doesn't feel like that. How do you even start talking about God in an age when transcendence is looked upon with such suspicion?

I remember a discussion in my school during one of our INSET days on Catholic ethos. We were considering the question of religious decline in the western world and one of our colleagues, who comes from Zimbabwe, said that our problem was that we did not need God. In her country, with chronic corruption, violence, poverty and oppression, the cross meant something, and gathering together in community for Mass felt more like a necessity than one option among many on a Sunday morning. For us in the rich west (and despite the deprivation in our society we are a very wealthy country) God seems lost in a dead language. There's no real sense any more of stepping from domestic space into sacred space. When we went to Church years ago you knew you were in a different sort of place and you behaved accordingly. For most people today there's a kind of continuum of informality that runs through home – school – shopping mall. There may be slightly different norms of behaviour expected but there's no sense of stepping out of time. I think we would be doing our young people a great service by restoring something of the sense of the sacred we were brought up with – that deep incense-laden peace you may remember at benediction. We cannot give up on this, even if our young people kick against silence. In a later chapter we will look at the idea of sacred time, as well as sacred space.

If it is challenging today to convince young people that their identity depends on God, our other fundamental assumptions about identity are also being challenged. The Equalities Act of 2010 made it unlawful to discriminate against people with "protected characteristics". There are nine such characteristics: age; disability; gender reassignment; marriage and civil partnership; pregnancy and maternity; race; religion or belief; sex; sexual orientation. Some of these go to the very heart of what we have for generations considered to be part of a shared understanding of identity, such as gender reassignment. I have had recent experience as a headteacher of a young person who wished to finish one school year as a girl and begin the next as a boy, without any medical procedures. I was initially at a loss as to how to respond, but as I have learned to do over the years, I took time to take advice. I was most encouraged by the attitude of the Church; the formal and informal advice I received was very much about caring for the young person, being with him or her on their journey, and making sure that everyone around him or her was invited into a deeper understanding of his or her needs. Our challenges may become more complex, but the source of our guidance and inspiration remains constant and faithful.

For a more sustained reading of modernity and how the Catholic Church needs to engage with the concerns of the people of this age, as requested by Vatican II, I would recommend another of our buried gems, *On the Way to Life*. This document was produced in 2005 by the Jesuits at the Heythrop Institute for Religion, Ethics and Public Life in London.[19] There was a brief period of excitement following its publication, as it was seen to be a breakthrough engagement with the modern age, but sadly the momentum drained away amidst unfortunate comments about being overly academic. It is not an easy read but it is very worthwhile.

PAUSE AND REFLECT

- How do we help our young people to find their identity in the divine?

To Discern

The final attitude is the process of discernment, which is the effective choice of the young person. This may come when they are older, but seeds can be sown at any age. On the Road to Emmaus the moment when the two disciples rose at "that same hour" is seen as the moment of discernment and decision. They know, not just what they have to do, but who they are. The return to Jerusalem is like a return home; there's a sense of rightness in the choice, which is familiar to anyone whose life is in tune with their vocation. Those of us who lead secondary schools especially will know that not every sixteen- or eighteen-year old can articulate what they want to do, and sometimes we expect too much from our young people in our endless probing at their profiles and possible options for the future. We must be careful not to oversimplify vocation.

The other thing I wanted to be at the age of ten was a priest and duly went off to junior seminary to become one. I was there until I was nineteen and then spent several years feeling very lost until I became a teacher, which felt like a new vocation, or rather a new understanding of my original vocation. But then I became a headteacher and mostly stopped teaching, so what had happened to my vocation? And if my vocation is now headship, what will become of that when I am no longer a headteacher? What may help us here is the insight that our fundamental vocation to love and holiness is like a baseline running through our lives. At different times there will be different manifestations of that vocation in different roles, or different types of work, different motifs if you like. We also need to be careful not to over-associate vocation with a job, since that leaves those without work potentially excluded from vocation, which cannot be the case. One headteacher I met on my visits had developed a very insightful understanding of his vocation as follows:

Absolutely a hundred per cent it's a vocation, but for me vocation is the thing that you do that shines a light on your true identity, on who you are. If I had become a soldier, like my father was, I don't think it would have shone a light on who I truly am. How do I compensate for that when it's no longer there?

As I say, it's a means to an end. The job I do as a headteacher is a means towards my vocation, it's a second-order vocation and I suppose I just have to find ways of continuing to develop my identity and discover more about it which doesn't involve being a teacher.

Secondary Headteacher

Beyond the fundamental call, vocation can then be seen in the broader perspective of service that we started with, using our giftedness in the loving service of the Church or society for the common good:

In the lives of individuals, there exist various types of call: to life primarily, and then to love; to responsibility to the gift, then to faith; to following Jesus; to the particular witness of one's own faith; to being father or mother, and to a particular service for the Church or society. [20]

The pedagogical attitudes may provide Catholic leaders with a framework or at least some idea of how to make a culture of vocation a reality in schools.

In this country, the promotion of vocation in the deepest sense is seen as a priority of the Bishops' Conference. We have a National Office for Vocation, and our National Vocations Director, Fr Christopher Jamison OSB, is leading some innovative work with schools on how to make a culture of vocation an integral part of the curriculum. In a recent article he outlines the work he has done with one diocese developing a culture of vocation in the curriculum of our schools. The vision he describes is of a "vocational curriculum in the profoundest meaning of the word vocation"[21] in which every subject is called upon to show how people respond to the call of Christ. We are not talking here about some fundamentalist notion of Catholic maths and Catholic science, but a school culture in which teachers are confident to explore the spiritual and moral dimensions of the subject and to include examples of dedicated lives which contributed to the common good.

The notion of "some definite service", as expressed in the memorable prayer of Blessed John Henry Newman, has a long tradition and generations of men and women have used their gifts in ways which can be highlighted in our curriculum. In my own school, I have asked those who teach our specialist subjects, namely performing arts and science, to lead the way and ensure that the examples of people who lived dedicated lives in these subject areas are promoted and celebrated. These key figures can then be a feature of project work and assemblies, and the gifts and qualities which these lives exhibit can be held up as examples. The website of the National Office for Vocation is another very helpful resource for Catholic leaders who want to develop a genuine culture of vocation in their school. The article "What is a vocation?" ends with a quotation from Mother Teresa which, like most of her words, cuts through our tortuous search for definitions: "Many people mistake our work for vocation. Our vocation is the love of Jesus."[22]

The National Framework for Vocations, which can be found at **www.ukvocation.org**, is a broad framework and is not specifically designed for schools. The website has useful resources for schools, but there is much to be done before we can say we have a (new) culture of vocation in our schools. In my interviews

with children and young people ranging from Year Four to Year Thirteen, common themes were very much in evidence: they felt safe, supported, and encouraged to be the best they can be, but there is no consistent language of vocation in use, or a preferential option for pathways of service for the common good. They do not look to the lives of the saints as perhaps previous generations did for their role models. They are not aware of a particularly strong promotion of vocations to the priesthood and religious life, or other types of ministry.

At a conference in my diocese, Fr Jamison outlined the role of leadership in schools in promoting a culture of vocation. Firstly, we need to understand vocation in the terms described in "New Vocations". For many of us this requires new thinking. Secondly, we must communicate a culture of vocation in our schools. It should be part of our strategic thinking, part of our development priorities and, I would argue, part of our mission statement. Thirdly, we need to discern vocation and encourage all our colleagues and every team in our school to help the children and young people in our schools answer the question Pope Benedict asked them when he spoke at the Big Assembly in 2010: "What kind of person would you really like to be?"

People Like Me

I found an inspiring example of how to promote a culture of vocation in an inner city sixth form college. When the principal showed me round he pointed out framed photographs on the walls of many former students with quotations from them on what the college had meant to them and why they ended up in their current job. The former students spoke very powerfully of the values, support and encouragement they had received in the college and how those values had to varying degrees stayed with them and shaped their attitudes in adult life. The jobs represented a wide spectrum and could not all be described as obviously contributing to the common good, but as the principal pointed out to me it doesn't really matter what they are doing, within reason of course, but more how they were going about their adult lives.

The college community had gone through some very dark days, including the loss to knife crime of a student and the involvement of some of its students in the murder of another young person. It had learned the hard way the importance of consistently promoting a positive culture of contributing to the common good by taking Gospel values into wider society and following whatever path seemed best suited to students' gifts. Many former students came back to talk to the current cohort about vocational pathways and to encourage them to apply themselves to their studies.

I have often thought that we are asked to measure the impact of our education at precisely the wrong moment, that is when our students leave us, rather than when we really see the impact, which is often many years later. It takes us back to one of those pedagogical attitudes: we nurture the God-strewn seeds and cannot predict the fruits. It is a notable feature of any established school community that they keep in touch with their former pupils and students and by celebrating their lives with the current students we can truly see a culture of vocation in action. The fruits of this culture of vocation are well summed up in the words of one of

the former students of the sixth form college who is now a teacher in a UN refugee camp in Lebanon and an officer on the World Food Programme:

[My] college was a huge turning point for me. Like a lot of people from my background, even being the first generation to go to university was an achievement. However, the teachers here pushed me and encouraged me to dream big, believe in my potential and suggested that I applied to one of the best universities in the world. I thought, "People like me don't go to places like that!" but [my college] was the perfect environment to challenge all the barriers that sometimes limit us. I had all the resources, all the support and all the guidance to lift my own expectations and now I work at a global level.

1 *Evangelii Gaudium*, 9.
2 *In Verbo Tuo* "New Vocations for a New Europe", 11(a). Found at: http://www.vatican.va/roman_curia/congregations/ccatheduc/documents/rc_con_ccatheduc_doc_13021998_new-vocations_en.html.
3 Catholic Youth Ministry Federation, *Mapping the Terrain* (London: Catholic Youth Ministry Federation, 2009).
4 Dr R. Wilkins, "Interpreting the tradition", *Networking Magazine* (April 2014), p. 8.
5 *In Verbo Tuo*, 11(b).
6 Ibid., 11(c).
7 Anna Bressanin, "Generation cool: self-obsessed millennials having so much fun" (BBC News Magazine, 18 June 2013). Found at: http://www.bbc.co.uk/news/magazine-22915026, 6 August 2014.
8 *Evangelii Gaudium*, 64.
9 *In Verbo Tuo*, 13(a).
10 Ibid., 13.
11 Ibid., 13.
12 K. Robinson, *The Element* (London: Allen Lane, 2009), xi.
13 *In Verbo Tuo*, 17(a).
14 Ibid., 33(c).
15 Ibid., 34.
16 Ibid., 34(b).
17 Quoted in R. Waterfield, *On Listening* (London: Penguin Classics, 1992), p. 88.
18 *Evangelii Gaudium*, 170.
19 Heythrop Institute for Religion, Ethics and Public Life, *On the Way to Life* (London: Heythrop Institute for Religion, Ethics and Public Life, 2005).
20 *In Verbo Tuo*, 26(c).
21 C. Jamison OSB, *International Studies in Catholic Education* (Abingdon: Routledge, 2013), p. 15.
22 National Office for Vocation, "What is a vocation?". Found at: http://www.ukvocation.org/what-is-a-vocation, 23 May 2014.

CHAPTER 3

Mission Control – the View of Catholic Schools from the Centre

Pope Francis has called us to be bold in looking for new signs and symbols and, as Catholic schools, to make sure that central to our work of education is "the explicit proclamation of the Gospel".[1] The most public way in which we declare what we stand for is our mission statement.

Just by way of definition before we begin: a mission statement is different to the ethos statement. All foundation or voluntary schools were required by the 1998 School Standards and Framework Act to adopt an ethos statement. The Catholic Education Service recommended that Catholic schools adopted the same ethos statement, which should be found in your *Instrument of Government*. The ethos statement defines the basic purpose of the school; the mission statement is derived from that and will reflect the particular circumstances of the school, based on certain foundational principles and strategic context. In the 2007 edition of *Evaluating the Distinctive Nature of a Catholic School*, the National Board of Religious Inspectors and Advisers offered the following definition:

The mission statement provides the foundation for all school and colleges policies and practices, and its principles should inform planning and target-setting. It should be a point of reference for all aspects of evaluation. It is in the daily life and work of the school or college that essential indicators for the achievement of its mission may be identified.[2]

If we are to renew our sense of purpose in the light of the *Apostolic Exhortation* of Francis then reviewing our mission statement would be a good place to start. In the documents of the Church, there is nothing about how often you should do this. In my visits to schools there was certainly no consensus on the matter but it was generally the case that the arrival of a new headteacher prompted a review. After that it was very variable, with a number of colleagues admitting that another look at the mission statement was probably overdue. As Catholic headteachers, it often falls to us to lead the mission review.

Governors should be involved, in fact they should be central to the process. In the *Governors' Handbook* published by the Department for Education in May 2014, the first of the three core strategic functions for governing bodies is "Ensuring clarity of vision, ethos and strategic direction".[3] An essential piece of work for Catholic schools is to determine the

Catholic dimension of this core strategic function. The sibling book to this volume, with a focus on how to survive in leadership for governors, by Sister Judith Russi, will explore in much more depth the strategic role of governors in Catholic schools.

In twelve years in Catholic headship, my understanding of mission has grown and is still growing. It is not something you arrive with fully formed on day one. It matures along with your understanding of your role and vocation as a Catholic leader. To begin with it may feel like someone else's mission, if you just use the Church's guidance and "tweak" what was there before. As you get to know your school community and grow in wisdom of the mission of the Church, then you will take ownership of your school's mission and it will become part of your personal spirituality. I think that's why it is important to review your mission statement. I would certainly argue for a major review of the mission statement every five years, but a review of the effectiveness and impact of the mission of the school should be ongoing and at the very heart of the school's monitoring and evaluation programme. In this chapter we will be looking at the process by which that mission is expressed and reviewed as well as considering some examples from our schools. I will also look at some more of the rich resources the Church provides to help us understand the mission of the Catholic school.

The first aspect of mission I'd like to consider is academic achievement, which for some headteachers and governing bodies creates a dilemma between meeting the expectations of the State to deliver ever better outcomes, and the expectations of the

Church, which wants more than just academic results. Some of my darkest moments in headship have come on results days in August when I have sat with a few colleagues in my office clutching the "headline" GCSE figures and felt something like depression settle over me. I know that my colleagues in primary schools have had similar days. Your mind races ahead to the conversations to come with the governors, students, parents, colleagues, and the inspectors who will know your RAISEonline better than you do and won't be moved by your analysis of the one-off dip in results. You check the websites of local schools and your heart sinks at the "best ever results" messages which some of them seem to achieve every year. Is this what it is all about? Where is mission in all this? How do we reconcile the performance pressures of the current system and the eternal demands of our mission as Catholic schools?

I do not believe that a focus on academic performance and the mission of Catholic schools are incompatible. In this country, as I said earlier, Catholic schools began as a vehicle for social mobility, a means to help the industrial poor aspire to something better. I am a case in point. Like many of my generation from a working-class background, I was the first member of my family to go to university. My father would certainly have been capable of further study, but he left school at fifteen, as was expected of him, and became a journeyman electrician. But the Church has always wanted the best for and from its young people in education. In my Catholic primary school in the industrial East End of Greenock in the late 1960s and early 1970s, we were all expected to speak properly, spell correctly, add and subtract, look smart, behave ourselves and go to Mass, irrespective of our circumstances. Education was important, it would help us to *get on*. I parted company with my peer group for secondary education to go to junior seminary, but the message for them was equally aspirational and, thanks to a social policy which saw a huge increase in free higher education places, the doors were open to university.

As I discovered in my school days, the concept of the dignity of the individual is central to the Church's view of education. In our society, the dignity that comes from having the means to live free from ignorance and poverty is determined to a large extent by the skills and qualifications gained at school (although increasingly those qualifications on their own are no guarantee of anything). The Church has always believed in education and has always called for her teachers to provide the very best standard of education. The expectations of Catholic schools are clearly set out in Canon Law:

Directors of Catholic schools are to take care under the watchfulness of the local ordinary that the instruction which is given in them is at least as academically distinguished as that in the other schools of the area.

Canon 806.2[4]

I have had a few conversations with colleagues who seem to prefer the word "outstanding" to "distinguished" in that Canon. It may be to do with the English or American translations, as one colleague suggested, but in fact it would not matter much which word was used except that in England "outstanding" is an Ofsted category (in Wales, the top Estyn category is "excellent") subject to criteria change, whereas "distinguished" makes a more general qualitative point that those who attend Catholic schools should receive at least as good a deal as their peers in local schools.

The other point to bear in mind is that in the tradition of Catholic education, academic excellence was always pursued for a higher end: *AMDG*, as we used to write at the front of our books, *Ad Maiorem Dei Gloriam* – to the Greater Glory of God. This idea has probably shifted from the vertical to the horizontal plane in recent years, with an emphasis on personal growth and service for the common good, but there is still a constant theme running through the tradition that academic excellence is worth aspiring to as part of the greater mission of the Church.

In his 2002 study, which included interviews with around sixty Catholic secondary headteachers, Gerald Grace concluded:

The classic Catholic position that academic achievement finds its full meaning in the service of higher ends was still a strong feature of the expressed mission of many of the schools in this research. Mission statements might now be printed in larger and glossier prospectus packages than in the past, but they continued to use a traditional discourse of "holiness and learning".[5]

So I have never been too troubled with reconciling academic achievement with Catholic mission. It is true that there are profound challenges for Catholic schools in the means by which results are achieved. Many schools, for example, are tempted to deploy considerable resources to help students on the borderline of results thresholds, whether that's SATs Level 3/4 or GCSE C/D borderline. I fully understand that temptation. In an era of "floor targets" there is huge pressure to ensure that the headline percentages are healthy so that Ofsted will be able to award the school "good" or better for achievement. Catholic schools, especially secondary schools, will be increasingly vulnerable to falling rolls as denominational transport subsidy disappears from council budgets and a drop in Ofsted category could prove very damaging to the school's reputation. A canny focus on exam results for strategic reasons is completely understandable in my view. The challenge for Catholic leaders is to ensure that in our focus on thresholds we do not neglect any students, especially the poor and vulnerable, who do not come into any group supported by additional funding.

The schools I visited which serve deprived communities had no doubts at all about the importance of academic outcomes. A critical part of their mission was to raise the aspirations of their young people and ensure they left school with as much advantage as possible. One headteacher of an inner city secondary school explained it this way:

These children, wherever they are on their journey, and some of their journeys have been pretty awful, we take them as far forward as we can. I am looking for academic excellence because whatever I say aspirationally about how much we love them, they're going to leave here and they need the tools to be successful in a world that isn't very forgiving of them and actually isn't very welcoming of them. I need them to have the very, very best academic results.

Secondary Headteacher

A Catholic school's mission statement has to be sensitive to its context. We have a foundational set of principles which we have seen in the previous chapter, and in this chapter we will look at those principles in more detail. Some are non-negotiable, but the prominence of some over others will depend on the circumstances of your school. Your mission is situational, to some extent. When I first became a headteacher in 2002, the school I took charge of was in a "category". In those days it was called "challenging circumstances". For a variety of reasons the school found itself in trouble: results were poor, behaviour was not good, and staff morale was very low. The governors had put their faith in me to lead the community out of this situation. I was a rookie from an "outstanding" school in the leafy shires, and when the office door closed behind me on day one I looked around and thought – *What do I do now?*

I had very little experience of real challenge and was running on instinct. I did not have time to conduct a wide-ranging consultation with all the stakeholders on how our mission should be expressed. I did not even know what a stakeholder was. I had HMI coming in a month and we just had to get a move on or the school would sink. I came up with the motto "Excellence for the sake of the Gospel", which seemed to strike the right chord and that became the foundation of our mission statement. Then came the carpets, the blazers, and the behaviour policy, and with supportive staff and a governing body who wanted this to work, we got there.

I had great pleasure going back to the school in the course of my research. The motto was still there but the new head told me with a wry smile that nobody really knew what it meant and it was now being reviewed with the full involvement of governors, staff, students and parents. The school was graded "good" by Ofsted; they were over-subscribed, results were excellent, the confidence was palpable and the sun was shining. Whatever expression of mission they come up with will reflect where they are now and where they want to go next, which will be quite different to the anxious community I first encountered all those years ago.

An inner city primary school I visited provided an inspirational example of a mission which responded to the needs of its children. The headteacher told me that in the process of reviewing their mission a few years ago they started with a survey of the children's attitudes, aspirations and lifestyles. What they discovered shaped their mission: sixty per cent of the children had never seen the sea, forty per cent had never been to the city centre (which was five miles away) and none of them had played a musical instrument. This not only led to a mission statement which prioritised "life to the full" but resulted in a curriculum which provided day trips to the coast, visits to city centre galleries and instrumental lessons for all children. There was every other dimension you would expect of a vibrant Catholic school, such as excellent RE, worship, daily prayer and charity work, but the emphasis of the mission statement and priorities for the deployment of resources arose out of the situation of the children.

"The Catholic School"

I have suggested two documents which I feel not only capture the present moment of the Church but which will provide schools with a rich resource for mission review: "The Joy of the Gospel" and "New Vocations". In both you will find many references to Church thinking on education and the formation of the young. Pope Francis reminded us that, "God has already spoken, and there is nothing further that we need to know, which has not been revealed to us."[6] We've had the fullness of revelation; we're just trying to discern what it means for us in our time and place. The tradition of the Church is like a great symphony, with familiar themes or motifs weaving in and out of a central melody. In every Church document there will be echoes or explicit references to the tradition.

We are not making this up, and that is a great comfort and source of strength.

I remember once showing a fellow headteacher round my school. She was not a Catholic but was searching for a set of values which could unify her community. She was very envious of the strength and coherence of the values which had been given to us by our identity. She settled in the end on the Olympic values, which had great currency in this country around 2012, but I did wonder what would happen when the glow of that competition faded?

For those who are looking for a fuller treatment of the foundational principles to help them review the mission of their school I would recommend Gerald Grace's book *Catholic Schools: Mission, Markets and Morality* (2002) for an excellent summary of the regulative principles of Catholic education from the documents which have come from the Vatican since 1965. The National Board of Religious Inspectors and Advisers (NBRIA) also has a very helpful summary of what to include in any review of mission in *Evaluating the Distinctive Nature of a Catholic School* (2007), and the updated version of Monsignor Marcus Stock's publication *Christ at the Centre* provides a comprehensive and systematic framework for what Catholic schools should always be mindful of when they come to review their mission.

There is one other document I would like to draw your attention to which I think is invaluable when it comes to a review of mission: "The Catholic School", published in 1977 by the Sacred Congregation for Catholic Education[7], is the more detailed follow-on from the Vatican Council's general statement of

principles on education, "Declaration on Christian Education". In my small sample of interviews it was clear that Catholic headteachers have a very sound, indeed profound, sense of mission which is lived in their day-to-day experience of leadership. Many of them however will tell you rather sheepishly that they haven't read the Church documents on education, as if they were admitting to their parents that they hadn't been to Mass on Sunday. The reasons for this are the usual problems about workload, but there was also a feeling that many of the documents are not all that accessible and in some cases relevant to their context. They often relied on the good services of the local church, especially their diocese, to "translate" the best of the thinking for them.

I've chosen what I consider to be the most relevant quotations from "The Catholic School" for any leadership team or governing body starting the process of mission review and have added some commentary.

The Catholic school forms part of the saving mission of the Church, especially for education in the faith.
Paragraph 9

The school must begin from the principle that its educational programme is intentionally directed to the growth of the whole person.

Paragraph 29

This idea is developed further in subsequent Church documents. The vision of a rounded education – which pays attention to the spiritual, moral, social, cultural, mental and physical – is a priority in the Church's vision. Saint John Paul II would later call this a "human ecology". The focus on academic achievement, then, sits within a wider vision of the purpose of education, but is in no way relegated in importance.

Christ is the foundation of the whole educational enterprise in a Catholic school. His revelation gives new meaning to life and helps man to direct his thought, action and will according to the Gospel, making the beatitudes his norm of life.

Paragraph 34

Christ at the Centre provides guidance on the Gospel values which arise from the Beatitudes. We often speak of Gospel values but not all Catholic schools clearly articulate what they are and how they are lived and evaluated in practice.

The nobility of the task to which teachers are called demands that, in imitation of Christ, the only Teacher, they reveal the Christian message not only by word but also by every gesture of their behaviour. This is what makes the difference between a school whose education is permeated by the Christian spirit and one in which religion is only regarded as
an academic subject like any other.

Paragraph 43

In a previous chapter, I referred to the Catholic school's commitment to safeguarding. That phrase "by every gesture of their behaviour" could well find a place in your staff and governor code of conduct as a perfect illustration of what is expected of them. It is also a reminder that what we do is more important than any form of words, or as St Francis is supposed to have said: "Preach the Gospel, use words if you have to."

They [pupils] are to overcome their individualism and discover, in the light of faith, their specific vocation to live responsibly in a community with others.

Paragraph 45

Knowledge is not to be considered as a means of material prosperity and success, but as a call to serve and to be responsible for others.

Paragraph 56

The theme of service and vocation, which is so central to the Church's thinking on education, was developed at some length in Chapter Two.

The Catholic school has as its specific duty the complete Christian formation of its pupils, and this task is of special significance today because of the inadequacy of the family and society.

Paragraph 45

Remember that this very direct assessment of the state of the modern family was written in 1977, when we thought the Catholic family was relatively strong.

For those who are wondering about the pupils who aren't Catholic or Christian in the school, the document goes on to say:

Its [the school's] task is to form Christian men, and, by its teaching and witness, show non-Christians something of the mystery of Christ Who surpasses all human understanding.

Paragraph 47

… the school proper is an active force through the systematic formation of the pupils' critical faculties to bring them to a measure of self-control and the ability to choose freely and conscientiously in the face of what is offered by the organs of social communication.

Paragraph 48

The document doesn't imagine a scenario when the pupils' newly mature critical faculties are turned on the Church, but that is something we also have to deal with, especially with older ones. In terms of pedagogy I see this priority translating into a culture of curiosity, exploration, debate and challenge in the classroom to facilitate the development of higher-order thinking.

Since it is motivated by the Christian ideal, the Catholic school is particularly sensitive to the call from every part of the world for a more just society, and it tries to make its own contribution towards it. It does not stop at the courageous teaching of the demands of justice even in the face of local opposition, but tries to put these demands into practice in its own community in the daily life of the school.

Paragraph 58

I think that's what Francis means by "make some noise"! – a call to work boldly for social justice, at home and abroad. More dioceses now seem to be emphasising the need to be just as focused on the injustice on our doorstep, which is often not as visible as the obvious poverty in some other countries.

First and foremost the Church offers its educational service to "the poor or those who are deprived of family help and affection or those who are far from the faith".

Paragraph 58

This is a reiteration of one of the great principles of Catholic education outlined in the "Declaration on Christian Education", published in 1965. Those who are poor must be our priority.

A policy of working for the common good is undertaken seriously as working for the building up of the Kingdom of God.

Paragraph 60

This is another expression of the theme of working for justice to ensure that all people have the means to live dignified lives, a theme Francis has taken us back to so strongly.[8]

The validity of the educational results of a Catholic school, however, cannot be measured by immediate efficiency… It is when the Catholic school adds its weight, consciously and overtly, to the liberating power of grace, that it becomes the Christian leaven in the world.

Paragraph 84

That one makes me somewhat nervous. I prefer the blatant encouragement of Canon 806. The point is that not everything can be measured, but that does not lessen the importance of academic outcomes, as discussed above.

In the certainty that the Spirit is at work in every person, the Catholic school offers itself to all, non-Christians included, with all its distinctive aims and means, acknowledging, preserving and promoting the spiritual and moral qualities, the social and cultural values, which characterise different civilisations.

Paragraph 85

This is a powerful summary of the great theology of nature and grace which informs Vatican II and should also provide us with the foundation for a positive view of the modern world. There is a foreshadowing too of the multicultural environment many of us now take for granted. It is also an interesting comment on the vexed question (in some dioceses) of the identity of the Catholic school due to the proportion of Catholic pupils. The message is pretty clear. It is not and never has been a numbers game. Catholic schools are invited to welcome those who have not been baptised, in the sure knowledge that the Spirit is at work in their hearts. We are invited to show them the love of God in the way that we care for them and accompany them on their journey.

The only condition it would make, as is its right, for its continued existence would be remaining faithful to the educational aims of the Catholic school.

Paragraph 86

Now if you included all of the above in your new mission statement, and the best thinking from "The Joy of the Gospel" and "New Vocations", and your own bishop's pastoral priorities, the vision of your founders, or the charism of your religious order, you'd have a bit of a tome. I have argued that each school's mission statement has to be responsive to its present circumstances and priorities. The points above are helpful in the definition of a Catholic school, but which of them any Catholic school chooses to highlight to its community will be a matter of prayerful discernment.

In summary, I think there are six key principles which we need to consider as part of our mission review, but how they are expressed or prioritised is a matter for the school in communion with its bishop or founders:

- Jesus Christ is our foundation – Gospel values as expressed in the Beatitudes are our touchstone.

- Our schools have a preferential option for those who are poor and vulnerable.

- We offer a rounded education – the growth of all aspects of the person, especially in faith.

- We promote a culture of vocation – recognising and developing the *original gift* in our young people.

- We prepare our young people for service in the common good – the transformation of society.

- We aim for academic excellence for the sake of the dignity of the individual.

Gospel Values

Many people in Catholic leadership speak of Gospel values as being at the heart of their mission, but do we know what we mean by that? We have already seen that the Church invites us to find the best definition of Gospel values in the Beatitudes. In *Christ at the Centre*, Monsignor Marcus Stock takes the Beatitudes from Matthew's Gospel (5:3-12) and defines the values as follows:

"Blessed are the poor in spirit, for theirs is the kingdom of heaven". Values: *faithfulness and integrity*.

"Blessed are those who mourn, for they shall be comforted." Values: *dignity and compassion*.

"Blessed are the meek, for they shall inherit the earth." Values: *humility and gentleness*.

"Blessed are those who hunger and thirst for righteousness, for they shall be satisfied." Values: *truth and justice*.

"Blessed are the merciful, for they shall obtain mercy." Values: *forgiveness and mercy*.

"Blessed are the pure in heart, for they will see God." Values: *purity and holiness*.

"Blessed are the peacemakers, for they shall be called children of God." Values: *tolerance and peace*.

"Blessed are those who are persecuted for righteousness' sake, for theirs is the kingdom of heaven. Blessed are you when they insult you and persecute you and utter every kind of slander against you because of me. Be glad and rejoice for your reward is great in heaven; they persecuted the prophets before you in the same way." Values: *service and sacrifice*.[9]

Monsignor Stock reminds us that "these Gospel values should constitute the targets and outcomes of the educational enterprise in every Catholic school". He goes on to say that for this to be achieved "these Gospel values need to be explicitly named, their meaning unpacked and pupils helped to understand how they relate to their lives…". He also makes the point which has been developed above that "this enterprise is not in addition to the quest for high academic standards and vocational excellence but integral to it".[10] *Christ at the Centre* does not "unpack" the Gospel values, but confirms where we should start. It is probably the work of a whole other book to explore in depth what Gospel values mean in the day-to-day running of a Catholic school, but it is essential work for Catholic schools and dioceses.

For any Catholic leader embarking on a study of Gospel values I would also recommend Richard Rohr's *Jesus' Plan for a New World*. Rohr reminds us that we have become accustomed to the Gospels and the sayings of Jesus to the extent that we are often deaf to the extraordinarily radical message. In the Gospels, and especially in the Sermon on the Mount (which contains the Beatitudes), we do not hear conventional wisdom, or rather we do hear conventional wisdom but only for it to be subverted by the wisdom of the Reign of God. "You have heard it said" is the formula Jesus uses to summarise the wisdom of the age before he says "but I say this to you…" to make it clear that his vision is not the vision of the world. Rohr sums up the message of the Sermon on the Mount as follows:

It is all about union and communion, it seems, which means that it is also about forgiveness, letting go, service and lives of patience and simplicity. Who can doubt that this is the sum and substance of Jesus' teaching? He makes right relationship desirable, possible and the philosopher's stone by which everything else is to be weighed and judged.[11]

Rohr's insistence that we have often missed the truth hidden in plain sight that Christianity is a *lifestyle* to which many in the Church have not subscribed is very close to the message of Pope Francis, who wants to bring us back to the essentials of the Gospel. We have heard many voices over the years calling us back to the core message, the purpose of our enterprise. Gerald Grace has kept Catholic headteachers and governors focused on the concept of "mission integrity", which is a similar invitation never to lose sight of the fundamental point that we must *live* what we say and avoid the drift towards rhetoric and gloss:

Mission integrity means that an organisation and the people within it can be seen to be living and practising the principles of the mission statement and not simply publishing them in a prospectus or in other publicity statements, as an exercise in marketing. The chief guardian of mission integrity is the school headteacher, which is why headteachers are leaders first and managers second.[12]

In the sibling book to this volume, Sister Judith Russi argues that the governors of Catholic schools are the guardians of the vision, which at first seems to contradict Grace's view that the headteacher is central to preserving mission integrity. From my experience as a practitioner, I think it is the headteacher who is the chief guardian of the mission on an operational basis, the faith leader on the front line, quite simply because he or she is the daily presence who often sets the tone and determines by his or her example what is important and what is not. The challenge of the headteacher, supported by the governors, is to create a climate in which everyone (ambitious, I know, but that has to be the aspiration) in the community understands the mission, their role in that mission, and lives that understanding in their daily routine.

It is not just Catholic schools who are interested in mission statements. It has become the norm in the commercial sector. The study of leadership and management is big business, with many theories about how to make and sustain successful organisations, but one of the most intuitive points which is consistently supported by the leaders in this field is that any successful organisation needs a common purpose, a shared mission. Stephen Covey, in *The Seven Habits of Highly Effective People*, tells the story of his visit to a hotel where he was delivering some training. He was enormously impressed by the level of service he encountered from every single member of staff he came across. Being in the business of mission statements, he wanted to know the secret. He interviewed some staff and was impressed by the extent to which they had taken on the "mission" of the hotel – *Uncompromising Personalised Service* – displayed prominently in all the staff areas. He asked the manager what was the key to success:

"Do you want to know the real key?" he enquired. He pulled out the mission statement for the hotel chain. After reading it, I acknowledged, "That's an impressive statement. But I know many companies have impressive mission statements." "Do you want to see the one for this hotel?" he asked. "Do you mean you developed one just for this hotel?" "Yes." "Different from the one for the hotel chain?" "Yes. It's in harmony with that statement, but this one pertains to our situation, our environment, our time." He handed me another paper. "Who developed this mission statement?" I asked. "Everybody," he replied. "Everybody? Really, everybody?" "Yes." "Housekeepers?" "Yes." "Waitresses?" "Yes." "Desk clerks?" "Yes." "Do you want to see the mission statement written by the people who greeted you last night?" He pulled out a mission statement that they, themselves, had written that was interwoven with all the other mission statements. Everyone, at every level, was involved. [13]

[1] *Evangelii Gaudium*, 134.
[2] National Board of Religious Inspectors and Advisers, *Evaluating the Distinctive Nature of a Catholic School* (National Board of Religious Inspectors and Advisers, 2007), p. 8.
[3] Department for Education, *Governors' Handbook* (Department for Education, May 2014), p. 7.
[4] Code of Canon Law, 806.2. Found at: www.vatican.va
[5] G. Grace, *Catholic Schools: Mission, Markets and Morality* (Abingdon: Routledge Falmer, 2002), p. 131.
[6] *Evangelii Gaudium*, 175.
[6] M. Stock, *Christ at the Centre* (London: Catholic Truth Society, 2012), p. 16.
[7] The Sacred Congregation for Catholic Education, "The Catholic school". Found at: www.vatican.va
[8] The Bishops of England and Wales developed this theme for our context in the inspiring document, "The common good", published in 1996.
[9] Stock, 2012, p. 17.
[10] Ibid., p. 17.
[11] R. Rohr with J. Feister, *Jesus' Plan for a New World* (Cincinnati: St Anthony Messenger Press, 1996), p. 11.
[12] G. Grace, "Catholic schools are now facing their greatest ever challenges", *Networking*, 9(4), 10.
[13] S. Covey, *The Seven Habits of Highly Effective People* (London: Simon and Schuster, 2004), p. 141.

CHAPTER 4

Mission Leadership – the View from the Bridge

Everybody needs to be involved but somebody has to take a lead and get the process started. Best practice in this respect would be the headteacher and the governing body working together to review where the school is on its journey and where it needs to get to. In secular language, this kind of evaluation should lead to an agreed understanding of *strategic intent*. In our terms we might call it *strategic mission intent*: What's the big picture? What kind of direction does this school need right now? That initial reflection often falls to the headteacher and the INSET day on Catholic ethos (which should be once a year) is often where he or she outlines the way forward for the school. I have been in my current school for ten years and we have just embarked on our third major review of mission. It started with an INSET day and a keynote presentation from me, talking about Francis, then "New Vocations", then revisiting the foundational themes in Catholic thinking on education. All members of staff were present (well most – one or two managed not to be there) and when I had finished my input I asked them to consider the following questions in their teams:

- How can your team better support the poor and vulnerable in the school?

- How can your team promote a culture of vocation or finding the "original gift" in our young people?

- Do you have any thoughts on how we can most effectively review our mission?

Because the staff were well used to these kinds of discussions, we had a high level of thoughtful engagement, with some challenging questions. One of the first things I learned in leadership was not to ask the question if you don't think you'll like the answer. Sometimes you need to be open, not defensive, and listen to what people are saying about the reality in the school. I knew there were concerns among the student support team about the fact that we had not succeeded in appointing a permanent SENCO after several attempts. Instead of going round all the teams during the discussions I stayed with them and let them share their concerns. It didn't solve anything but I think it showed that I considered the care of our students with special educational needs and disabilities to be at the heart of our mission and I told them that I would continue this conversation with them throughout the mission review.

We did not produce a mission statement that day. I said from the outset that the process would take many months and involve everybody. Just how any final mission statement is arrived at is a matter for each school according to its priorities. In the best examples I have seen there is some kind of "mission

team" – consisting of representatives from across the community, including of course students and governors – to lead the process. A key outcome is the production of a mission statement but it is also important to use the creativity of the community to ask in what ways can the mission of the school be seen, expressed and celebrated?

The great danger of mission review is that it is seen solely as a top-down process which has no bearing on the reality of the school. It is therefore critical, as we saw in the example from Covey at the end of the previous chapter, that all teams in the school are invited to produce their own version of the mission. In my school each faculty has its own mission statement which develops the understanding of mission according to their subject area. The physical education staff, for example, are able to focus on respect for the body and physical well-being, and can

articulate a mission philosophy of "taking part", each according to his or her ability. Science on the other hand may focus on the wonder of the created world and the role of curiosity and practical experimentation to help us discover its mystery. Each classroom can then have a statement which spells out what the mission looks like in *this* classroom and what the expectations are for staff and students.

It is not of course just subject teams who need to be involved in this process. As Covey discovered, every team should have a version of the mission, so that should include the reception team, the site team, the catering team, everybody. It is skilled work to lead teams through this, especially if they are uncomfortable with such open conversation about faith and mission, but they have signed up to work in a Catholic school so it shouldn't come as a complete surprise to be asked to reflect on what that means.

One of the biggest challenges we face in Catholic education is not only that more and more of our children and young people are unfamiliar with even the basic tenets of Christianity, but that the same can by said of our staff. The authors of *On the Way to Life* (see Chapter Two) refer to a "crisis of transmission" to describe the chronic weakening of the structures by which the faith tradition was handed down in previous generations, especially the family and the parish. The staff in our schools are often drawn to a faith environment for reasons they cannot always explain themselves, but we cannot take for granted what they know about the Catholic Church or the Christian faith.

Attention must be paid to their formation. This of course can be problematic since some will argue that they didn't join the school to be subjected to subtle attempts at conversion. Again, it's not a numbers game, but it is about inviting the adults in the community into a deeper personal understanding of what the Catholic school is all about. The outcomes of this process are very difficult to measure. We need biblical language for this work of the Spirit, not the empirical language of the age. We are nurturing seeds, as invited by "New Vocations", and patiently creating an environment where the seeds of faith can grow.

In the INSET day I mentioned above, one of my colleagues showed a film she had made in which around twenty members of staff from all teams in the school reflected on their own faith journeys and what it meant to them to work in a Catholic school. It was moving, open, honest and very powerful. It gave permission for everyone else to be open about their experience. We also held a question-and-answer session on working in a Catholic school and encouraged any questions, even on the so-called tricky topics or darker aspects of the experience of the Church in recent years. I did not feel any pressure to have all the answers, but I felt that inviting the questions was very much in line with the era of Pope Francis and where the Church is calling us to be at this time.

The individual formation of staff will have a collective dimension, but this kind of formation is more effective when it is *personalised*. We are all at very different points on our journey. In our school, for a number of years now, each member of staff has been asked to have a "mission objective" as part of their annual appraisal process. This is a "soft" objective, in that there is no salary or advancement riding on the outcome. There is no reprimand if the objective is not achieved – it is simply another way to invite each colleague to grow deeper in their own understanding of how to live the mission of the school.

Examples of objectives over the years have included support staff attending school Mass or liturgy which they don't normally have a chance to, or colleagues visiting other schools to see their chaplaincy in action, or joining a class visit to the local monastic foundation. The most effective examples of the personalisation of staff formation, however, are probably those thousands of conversations that take place in schools every day between colleagues, those encounters with people, when they are listened to, perhaps advice is given, and seeds are sown. Making time for those encounters is not easy in the school day, but we should never underestimate their impact.

In my experience parents are often left out of the process of mission review. We have a Parents' Forum which meets six times a year and the agenda is set by the parents. When we are in a period of more intensive mission review I will ask the parents to devote a meeting to consideration of our mission: Does it make sense to them? How can they support it? It is often uncomfortable territory for parents who consider this to be the school's job, but I think we have a significant piece of work to do to engage parents much more fully in mission thinking. It is part of the same issue of transmission which applies to students and staff. It will of course depend on the community and which part of the country you are in, but my feeling is that our outreach to parents is part of the evangelising role of the Church and involving them more fully and creatively in mission thinking is part of that.

As far as students are concerned, there are probably a few big decisions to make. Do you want the adults in the community to draw up the mission statement or mission programme and then ask the students to produce their own version, or do you want to be braver than that and involve them from the very beginning and allow them to shape the mission statement? Again, it will depend on the type of school, where the school is on its journey, and probably the age of the young people. In the examples that follow, you will find a mission statement from a primary school I visited which had a memorable pupil version: "To live, love and learn like Jesus". The statement was everywhere around the school and was very much part of the language of the children. It also proved to be a very powerful guide in deciding if any sort of behaviour was acceptable or not. The children, as far

as I could see, had not been involved in the writing of the statement but they very much "owned" it in their daily experience of the school. In another primary school I visited I asked the pupils, ranging from Years Four to Six, if they could tell me about their mission statement. They all looked at each for a second and then one said, "Shall we say it?" "Please do," I replied and then they recited their mission statement by heart as they did at assembly every Monday morning. That is what I call being on message.

The Church is often accused of a top-down paternalistic approach, but I think it would be unreasonable to expect children to lead an understanding of the mission of the Catholic school. There always has been a role for leaders or elders in the Church, the wisdom bearers. In my view we need to teach our children what the Church expects of its schools and then ask them for help in expressing that mission in ways which answer the present needs and circumstances. We cannot forget the obvious point that it is all about them, nor can we forget our responsibility to lead them in wisdom. Below, I have outlined one example from my own experience of how student voice might be used in the process of mission review.

Student Voice

In a Catholic school I believe that student voice is a very real way in which the community can put into practice the foundational belief in the dignity of the individual or, as Pope Francis put it, the "sacred grandeur" of our brothers and sisters (for more on this see Chapter One). There are many ways to make this a reality, but one format I have developed over the years is the "mission conference". This can be done in any way to suit the circumstances of your school, but in our secondary school we take a year group (around a hundred and sixty students) at a time and take them off timetable for a double lesson (around a hundred minutes). In a primary school, this could be a class group. The students are with their form tutors throughout, not their normal teachers. It has implications for cover and time out of normal lessons, but staff understand that in a Catholic school such activities are fundamentally important. The main purpose of such an exercise is for the students to engage with the mission of the school and to produce their own version of the mission statement or a student creed. Despite all that has been said about young people's lack of participation in the life of the Church, they still have a strong attachment to the values of the Church and are more than happy to see their version of those values writ large around the school.

We start in the hall with a plenary which I normally lead. This role doesn't have to be taken by the headteacher, but I think it sends a very strong signal to the students and the staff that this is an important activity. And, of course, as a number of headteachers have pointed out to me, in any assembly you are talking as much to the people around the edges of the hall, that is, your staff. It is all part of their formation to hear you articulating mission to different audiences. So I provide some introduction to the idea of mission, with some references to corporate mottos to try and establish what mission is all about. I then remind them of some of the non-negotiable aspects of the mission of a Catholic school which we've looked at above (for more about this turn to Chapter Two). When I do this as part of our current mission

review I spend time talking about Francis and what he has called us to consider as being essential. We finally look at our own context and I remind the students of our current priorities. In my diocese, for example, next year will be a Year of Vocation, so I will make sure that that features strongly in our current mission review. Many Catholic schools have a particular charism deriving from their foundation, perhaps in one of the religious orders of the Church. The final part of the opening plenary is to establish no more than three key questions the students will go off and discuss with their tutors:

- What do we do well as a Catholic school?

- What could we do better?

- What key phrases or ideas would you like to see in a student creed, or mission statement?

You will need to brief the tutors beforehand, but any skilled teacher will be able to run a discussion group of this kind. In most cases, the tutors divide the students into smaller discussion groups and nominate a boy and girl to give the feedback to the year group. Allow a good thirty minutes for this discussion and then get them all back in the hall. It adds to the fun of it all to have the feedback filmed. Then ask the representatives from each tutor group to come up to the front, give them the microphone and the floor.

I've had a few tense moments during feedback when the students have almost strayed into dangerous territory, but by and large they will respect this opportunity and the rule about not embarrassing anybody. The mission team then work with you to write up the final creed or statement by the students. When you have your student creed it's important that it doesn't become a trophy which is kept under glass and produced only for the annual prize-giving. It can be used prayerfully in school Masses or liturgies, there could be versions of it on display in the classroom and corridors and, better still, there could be questions drawn up by the students to make sure it is being lived in the daily experience of the school. That is a whole new level of accountability but many schools are developing similar models. We know instinctively that a crucial dimension of our mission as Catholic schools is to provide our children and young people with the dignity of a voice and to take seriously what they say. Experience tells us how to manage that voice, which is important, since there are still some colleagues who are very suspicious of student voice and fearful of its consequences.

In my visits to schools and colleges in the maintained and independent sectors, I asked groups of students to try and sum up their school in a few words. Here are some of their answers:

In the hall it says "Live, Love and Learn like Jesus" and then the younger children look at it and they might not really know what it means and then the older children are meant to be listening and living, loving and learning like Jesus, so the younger children look at the older children and realise what it means.
Year Six Student

It's quite obvious that there's something that isn't just day to day, there's something behind it all.
Year Six Student

It's a close-knit school where God is at the centre and we strive for academic excellence.
Year Thirteen Student

It's really helped me to grow in confidence and actually faith, it's really helped me to establish that it's what I want and not just what my parents want.
Year Thirteen Student

Care, effort and kindness.
Year Ten Student

Everyone wants the best for you.
Year Eleven Student

A way of life through Christ.
Year Ten Student

The students to be interviewed during my visits were picked by the schools, so they were probably already on board, but it was nevertheless clear to me that in

Catholic schools there is a high level of "ownership" by the students when it comes to understanding the mission.

Mission Review – Keep it Real

Once the mission statement has been approved by the governing body and each team has its own version of it and there is a students' version which is prominently displayed around the school, it is important to ensure that it does not merely become an exhibit in reception with no real bearing on how the school operates. When a clear sense of mission has been established, everything else should flow from it and be informed by it. The *School Development Plan* is where most schools spell out their strategic and operational objectives. In a Catholic school, the SDP should begin with the mission statement which should in turn inform the priorities. There is a key role here for the headteacher and governors to ensure that this is how it works in practice. The school's leadership should also ensure that every policy begins with an expression of mission. For a Catholic school it should not be difficult to see the connections between supporting those on "pupil premium" (for more on this see Chapter One), safeguarding, or health and safety with the foundational priorities expected by the Church.

The mission should be the first point of entry for all those who visit the school, either physically or online. Is the mission clearly signposted on the website and in reception? More importantly, is the mission evident in the first encounters with the staff of the school? When it comes to the selection process for new appointments there needs to be a clear understanding right from the initial letter to the enquirer about what the school stands for and what the expectations are for those who work there or wish to work in the school. Many schools now use the Catholic Education Service (England and Wales) contracts of employment and send a copy out to candidates prior to interview. In the interview of course there will be questions about how the colleague will support the ethos and mission in his or her capacity as a teacher or member of the support staff. This question often causes difficulty and I have to say is often answered very poorly by Catholic candidates, who seem unused to reflecting on what their faith means to them.

The next crucial aspect of the process is mission review. Very good schools keep asking themselves the question: How are we doing? This question applies to every aspect of the work of the school but should apply most of all to the mission. Some teams may argue that they simply do not have the time to put a mission review on their agenda, but I would say that at least once a year each team in the school should confront the questions: How have we lived up to our mission this year? How can we deepen our commitment to mission? The answers should inform the next round of planning. The teams, which should lead this process by example of course, are the senior leadership team and the full governing body. At least once a year, the minutes of both these teams' meetings should reflect an honest and professional scrutiny of the extent to which the school has lived out its stated mission. Where are the strengths? Are we celebrating them? What are the areas for development? What are we doing about them?

Mission Statements – Some Examples

Primary School (maintained)

"Our mission in [School Name] is to develop each child's talents and potential in a caring Catholic community inspired by the teaching of Jesus Christ."

"Live, love and learn like Jesus."
Pupils' version of the mission statement

Sixth Form College

Mission Statement

The College's mission is to enable all its students to achieve their **greatest potential**, inspiring them to **wisdom**, **compassion** and **leadership** in **service to others**. We aim to achieve this in a community defined by **Catholic values** which has the **person and teaching of Christ** at its **centre**.

Preparatory School (co-ed, independent)

"Our mission is to provide a secure and happy environment where children will develop the inner confidence necessary to flourish in a rapidly changing world. Whilst we protect and nurture our children,

we also challenge and stretch them in order to build their ability to thrive as adults in the future. We strive to awaken the children – spiritually and emotionally – making sure that individual minds are broadened and perspectives widened. We encourage learning, independence of thought and the nurturing of self-belief, skill and wisdom. We are preparing the children for their future in the ever-changing world they are growing up in and the lives they will lead. We are nurturing each child and encouraging them to live responsibly and compassionately and to embrace, with energy and enthusiasm, the great opportunities that lie ahead. It is our sincere desire that each will use their passions, knowledge and energies to make the world a better place. We will always encourage our children to dream – as dreams can be the seeds of future knowledge and wisdom. We want them to have the inner confidence to dream out loud. When they leave us, it is our sincere hope that they continue to dream out loud, with passion and commitment and at high volume."

Secondary School (co-ed, academy)

"To create a Christ-centred learning community where every individual is enabled to fulfil their true potential."

Primary School (maintained)

"Through Faith and education, [School Name] seeks 'fullness of life' for all members of the school community."

Secondary School (co-ed, academy)

"Our mission is to provide a rigorous and broad education within the context of a Christian environment. *An understanding of the Roman Catholic faith, in line with the Gospel message, underpins the whole work of the school. Our main aim is to develop the self-esteem, dignity and respect of all members of the community by concentrating on each person's infinite worth in the eyes of God."*

St Scholastica's, Manila (secondary, girls, independent)

One of the emerging themes of this study is that the Church is entering a new global era. In a later chapter I will look in more detail at what a global perspective might teach us. It is salutary for us when considering mission to look at how some schools in the less economically developed countries view their mission. One of the temptations we face is to pathologise communities in the developing world and regard them as objects of our charity. That is a mistake. We must learn from them and create a culture of interdependence. Sr Mary John Mananzan, whose work we will look at in more detail later on, was the principal of St Scholastica's private school for girls in Manila, the capital of the Philippines. When she was asked by a colleague of mine at a recent conference what the purpose of the school was she replied without hesitation: "social transformation". St Scholastica's is an independent school but the purpose of the education is to inspire the girls to challenge and transform society, *literally*: they frequently take to the streets to protest. On the homepage of their website (**www.ssc.edu.ph**) the school theme for 2012-2015 is the first thing you see:

Christ-Centred Leaders, Renewing our Culture, Revitalizing our Community,

Restoring the Integrity of Mother Earth with Joy and Hope.

The sense of mission authority in that statement is inspiring. There is a much bigger study to be undertaken to see our schools in a global context and for us to learn from the energy and vision of schools from the so-called developing world. St Scholastica's school theme reflects their context. It is interesting to note that there is no mention of personal growth or potential. It is all about Christ, leadership, culture, community and the earth. In the mission statements from my research above, which are fairly typical of the sixteen schools I visited, there is also a clear focus on Christ at the centre of the educational enterprise, but there is more emphasis on the growth and potential of the individual, which is perhaps more of a feature of the society we inhabit.

The Trojan Horse

The emphasis on the pursuit of academic excellence is more variable, depending on the circumstances and tradition of the school. There is not much explicit reference to the poor and vulnerable, but in my interviews with headteachers many thought this was not necessary in the outward-facing expression of mission, lest it made any section of their community feel labelled or defined by their economic circumstances. The main priority was to show in action that disadvantaged students were a priority when it came to distributing the resources of the school. Many schools will also have "aims" outlined beneath the public expression of mission which make the commitment to those who are poor and vulnerable evident.

There are few explicit references, apart from one school, to an education in the Catholic faith. Gerald Grace observed the variations of emphasis in this regard. According to his research: "some institutions were very clear that a serious engagement with the religious culture of the Roman Catholic Church was a prime aim of the school," while in other schools, "the aims of the mission statements tended to be expressed in more open and comprehensive terms."[1] It seems that this shift away from reference to education in the faith to an emphasis on Gospel and the growth of the individual is something of a pattern and probably reflects a response by Catholic schools to the wider shifts in society and the problems arising from the crisis of transmission.

The so-called "Trojan Horse" controversy of 2014 in some parts of England will perhaps ensure that this shift becomes more strategically motivated. Concerns were raised that in a number of community primary schools in one city there was a concerted effort by governors to promote a narrow interpretation of Islam. A report into these concerns by the Education Funding Agency said that the educational trust responsible for running three of the schools in question had not provided a broad and balanced curriculum; had not taken into account the guidance issued by the Secretary of State for Education with regards to sex and relationship education; and some elements of the social, moral, spiritual and cultural provision in the schools were restricted to a

conservative religious perspective. There are some very powerful groups in this country who want to see an end to faith schools. Some commentators have used the Trojan Horse issue to brand all faith-based education as potentially harmful.

The fact of the matter is that most of the schools involved in the controversy were community schools and should not have been pursuing a faith-based agenda. This fact has not been prominent in the media reports. The Catholic educational community may well feel under pressure to avoid any accusations of a narrowly faith-based education and focus instead on the broader themes which will find some sympathy in the anti-faith camp, such as the promotion of the human person, vocation, and the common good. A number of politicians have responded to this controversy by suggesting that the promotion of British values in our schools should be made compulsory. There will be much work in the coming years, I suspect, on the careful definition of those values. Whatever list we end up with (rule of law? fair play? tolerance? democracy?) Catholic schools will be faced with the question: To what extent are British values compatible with Gospel values? Whatever unfolds in the coming years, we can be confident in the values we hold dear, knowing that there is nothing which we believe in which is incompatible with human flourishing.

I asked each of the headteachers I visited if they would sum up their understanding of their school's mission. Here are some of their comments.

Catholic Headteachers on Mission

I still think that fundamentally what we hope to offer young people is a personal relationship with Christ because I think if we don't do that I can't quite see what's defining us as Catholic schools. I think another factor of the Catholic school of course is that we have this rather deep notion of communion, a communion of saints, which goes not only globally but also through time so we are a community that includes the dead, although no one's dead as far as God is concerned.

Secondary Headmaster, Religious Order

The thing that really strikes you when you've been here for a while and you get to know the school, it's about service to others. We say very clearly to prospective parents that at eighteen we want our young men and women when they leave here to look towards others first before themselves and that sense of service in a family, in a community, in an office, wherever it may be, is crucial.

Secondary Headmaster

I feel that society can't wait for our kids to get out there because they are fabulous, they need to be armed with the gifts of the Gospel values and the decency of how to basically treat people well. The world is waiting for these kids to come out and they have everything to offer. I know that's a little bit "rose-coloured spectacles" but I feel you can't be in education and be cynical.

Primary Headteacher

How I see it is, they learn about the Gospel, they learn about Christ, they learn about our Church and about the Catholic faith, the difficulty and probably one of the main challenges for the school is that some of them are learning this for the very first time. I think that is our biggest challenge, that we now have children who come to our schools whose fundamental knowledge of faith is not embedded in the family.

Primary Headteacher

To celebrate everything about young people and to give them confidence to go out into the world to deliver the message, the Gospel message of "everyone is special". I think Catholic schools have a much more difficult job nowadays because the students have got so much to deal with and some of them are not getting help from their parents. They say that Catholic schools are out-performing other schools on the whole but they're only talking about academic performance, they're not measuring how rounded a young person comes out.

Secondary Headteacher

It is quite remarkable how much of what the headteachers said when describing their mission found a resonance in "The Catholic School" – the Church document we discussed in Chapter Three – and yet only one of them (a member of a religious order) had read the document. We can perhaps account for this by the experience of their own Catholic education and upbringing but, given the "crisis of transmission", can we assume that an understanding of mission by osmosis will be a feature of future generations of Catholic leaders? And if mission thinking becomes attenuated, will we be vulnerable to those who are emboldened to seek an end to the existence of Catholic Schools?

Mission Review: a Ten-step Guide

Step	Action
1	Strategic review by head and governors: Where is the school at the moment? What are the strategic priorities moving forward? *Strategic intent*.
2	Review the foundational expectations of the Church for its Catholic schools, as well as any diocesan priorities, or expectations of the founders. *Mission foundation*.
3	What is the current mission statement? Is it fit for purpose? How successful has the school been in making its mission a reality? *Mission journey*.
4	Draw up a mission framework with the key principles and phrases which will inform the revised mission statement. *Strategic mission intent*.
5	All school teams to consider the main elements they would wish to have in their own version of the mission statement. *Mission ownership*.
6	Parents to be engaged in a forum. What does the current mission statement mean to them? How might it be improved? How might they support the mission? *Mission evangelisation*.
7	Pupils to be engaged – determine the extent of pupil engagement and leadership, perhaps working on their version of the mission statement. *Mission education*.
8	Governors agree the final mission statement and the statements from the teams and a mission policy, which outlines how the mission will be lived and reviewed. *Mission policy*.
9	All policies, induction, training and processes in school to be informed by the mission statement and subjected to the question: To what extent does this deepen our mission? *Mission process*.
10	Mission review to be undertaken once a year by every team, senior leadership, governors, parents and pupils – outcomes to be shared and used to inform planning. *Mission review*.

[1] G. Grace, *Catholic Schools: Mission, Markets and Morality* (Abingdon: Routledge Falmer, 2002), pp. 126-127.

CHAPTER 5

A Servant and a Leader

You're in post as a senior leader in a Catholic school or college because a group of people believed in you. Whether you were appointed last month, or ten years ago, the governing body, or trustees, made that decision based on a process of considerable scrutiny and they believe to this day that you are the person to lead the school. In this chapter we will look more closely at what is required of you and try and provide some insights and resources to sustain you on the road.

The literature on school leadership is considerable and the best of it is very worthwhile. But you are not just the leader of a school. You are the leader of a Catholic school and that requires another level of thinking. *Christ at the Centre* states that Catholic schools are distinctive when they, "model leadership inspired by the image of Christ."[1] We need to look in more depth at what this means. What kind of model of leadership does Jesus offer us? To answer that we have to look at where Jesus is revealed most fully to us: sacred scripture.

Catholics do not have an exemplary record when it comes to the reading and study of the scriptures. Within living memory, the word of God was read at Mass in a language few people could understand. There was no great engagement with the scriptures among lay people and there was little understanding of

how they came to be written. That changed dramatically with Vatican II. Following the liturgical reforms, the faithful could hear the readings in their own language, but more significantly, the scholarly work on the scriptures which had been underway for many years began to filter through. Catholic biblical scholars, such as the American Fr Raymond E. Brown, began to introduce to wider audiences the critical investigation of the Bible, which opened up for the first time the world in which the scriptures were produced and the intentions and context of the writers.

A tremor of this excitement was felt in a small living room in Greenock in the 1970s and 1980s. My father, a great student of Raymond E. Brown, taught himself the essentials of the new critical-historical method of reading scripture and started a study group in the parish. When I was home from seminary I joined them, sitting on the most uncomfortable chair, and was always impressed by the sincere efforts of those ordinary people to prayerfully understand what the word of God was saying to them.

It seems to me the excitement has waned since then and the great wisdom of Catholic scripture scholars has not made its way through to the mainstream of Catholic life. Most of the sixteen Catholic leaders I interviewed were brought up in traditional Catholic communities with a strong sense of transmission and

yet, as the leaders of Catholic learning communities, they generally did not have a working knowledge of the new ways of reading scripture. This to me suggests some deficiency in their formation as leaders which needs to be addressed. It also means that our children and young people could well be subjected to a literal, or fundamentalist, reading of scriptures (see the discussion of the Parable of the Talents in Chapter One).

In 1964 the Church gave its official blessing to the new method when the Pontifical Biblical Commission published the "Instruction on the Historical Truth of the Gospels". It is beyond the scope of this book to look in detail at this short but hugely significant paper. It is easily available online – for example at **www. catholicculture.org.** I would also recommend Raymond E. Brown's *The Critical Meaning of the Bible* as an excellent starting point for those wishing to understand the essentials of this approach.[2] For our purposes, I would like to focus briefly on the Gospel of Mark, which can be read as a very compelling portrait of Christian leadership at its most human.

The Gospel of Mark – a Portrait of Suffering Leadership

There are several theories about who the Gospel of Mark was written for, but a number of scholars suggest it was the Christian community in Rome around AD 70. If Mark was specifically addressing Roman Christians, he was writing for a community that had suffered great persecution and probably lived in a state of fear. For the last three years of Nero's reign (AD 65-68) being a Christian was a capital crime in Rome. The Christian community had been Nero's scapegoats for the great fire of Rome in July AD 64. They lived in fear of betrayal and it is suggested that Christians turned on other Christians, which may find an echo in Mark when it says, "Brother will betray brother to death, and a father his child, and children rise against parents and have them put to death" (Mark 13:12). Two of the apostolic pillars of the Church, Peter and Paul, were probably executed in Rome during the persecution, and in AD 70 the Temple in Jerusalem, which many early Christians still looked to as the centre of their faith, was destroyed by the Roman army. This was a broken and anxious community, which had lost its leaders and its symbolic centre (think of St Peter's in Rome for Catholics today) and was scarred by the vivid memories of persecution and betrayal, even within their own families.

When we then turn to the passion story in Mark, we can perhaps see why there is so much emphasis on pain and betrayal. The disciples do not come out of this scene well. Throughout the Gospel they are often portrayed as dull-witted, or simply "astounded" by events, and in the moment of trial in Gethsemane they disappear when they are most needed. There is an almost comical moment when the last disciple to flee is grabbed by the guards but leaves his linen cloth in their hands and "ran off naked" (Mark 14:52). What an image of discipleship: a bare backside vanishing into the night in utter panic, as may well have happened in first-century Rome during the persecutions.

The inner circle does not fare much better. It is interesting for today's leaders to note that throughout the Gospels Jesus seemed to work with a trusted few and confided in them at key moments. There is a psychological realism to this, which I'm sure will ring true with school leaders. In Gethsemane, at the moment of crisis, he took with him Ss Peter, James and John. A short time before, Ss James and John had been lobbying for the best places in glory, at the right and left of Jesus, which caused great unrest in the staffroom. At the Last Supper, Peter was vehement that even if everybody else lost faith in the strategic direction, he would not. A few hours later all three of them were heavy with sleep while Jesus grappled with his *agonia* alone. After the arrest, Peter denied that he knew Jesus when a young girl stared at him in the courtyard and accused him of being a follower – a scene which would surely have resonated nervously with the early Christian community in Rome.

The Gospel writers give significantly different accounts of the events of Gethsemane, which makes accurate reconstruction of what really happened difficult, but which reflects their own temperament and the communities for which they were writing. Mark shows Jesus in a state of acute distress. Such is the depth of his anxiety that he cannot remain upright.

He suffers a kind of postural collapse and falls to the ground. The trusted ones are heavy with sleep. There is no sign of comfort from *"Abba"*, his Father (a few hours later on the cross Jesus uses the more distant word *"Eloi"* to show the depth of abandonment).

Luke sends an angel to support Jesus in his version of Gethsemane; in Matthew's Gospel Jesus says that he could appeal to his Father to send twelve legions of angels, and by the time we get to John's Gospel, Jesus is the only one who is upright, with everyone else around him on their knees. But Mark is dark and stark. This is a leader on the very edge of his resources: broken, clueless and alone. We are so often beguiled by the rhetoric of relentless performance, the myth of perpetual effectiveness, the need to always look in control. But that is not the human experience, the experience of the Church, or the experience of Jesus.

If that were the final word then the universe would be a darkly comic place. For many in our times that is precisely the case and the portrait of leadership flat on its face is a staple of satire. But that can never be the final word for Christians. Mark does not have the haunting post-resurrection scenes of Luke and there is no reconciliation between Jesus and Peter, but there is resurrection. A young man in a white robe on Easter Sunday morning tells the women that Jesus has gone ahead of them to Galilee. There is hope, there is resurrection and in Luke's Gospel and in Acts, we see a broken community re-formed by the power of the Holy Spirit and sent out into the world with confidence. The Christian community in Rome will have seen that for themselves, with a forgiven Peter at the heart of things, preaching, leading and inspiring.

As Fr McBride, another student of Raymond E. Brown, explains in *Where Does the Jesus Story Begin?*:

In hearing the Gospel, Mark's community is helped to see that their own suffering, like the story of Jesus' suffering, is not some catastrophic mischance that is devoid of meaning, but a chronicle of salvation that rested within the prophecies of Jesus and God's providence. [3]

I think the Catholic tradition has an instinctive grasp, or folk memory, of the dark night of leadership. We have an established perception of the human condition as a mixed blessing. We know that we will suffer and fall. We hope it is not too public, too often, or beyond our capability to deal with, but *we will fall*; that is a given. It is what we do with our suffering that counts. We have faith in a leader who has suffered the full human experience, even as far as a violent death, and has been raised to glory. We have the hope of resurrection, which translates into the idioms of leadership as *resilience*.

Every headteacher I met spoke of tough days, dark times, occasionally verging on the impossible. In one school, there was nothing on the wall of the headteacher's office apart from a crucifix. When I asked him how he dealt with the more demanding times he said:

Spiritually there are a number of things. You turn to God. At the darkest moments I would turn to the cross up there and say, "Help me out here, I'm in real difficulty."
Primary Headteacher

We hope and pray that such moments are rare, but they are a feature of all leadership. The Christian tradition has a profound understanding of such moments and a firm belief that they are not pointless and not final.

Servant Leadership

In the Gospels Jesus makes it clear that for his disciples the worldly model of leadership has no place in the kingdom of God. In the scene from Mark 10 mentioned above, James and John start a row among the disciples by blatantly pitching for the top table in the kingdom – they want to be on the left and right of Jesus in glory. These are the "Sons of Thunder" after all, whose idea of a pastoral strategy for a community which didn't respond well to the message of Jesus was to incinerate them (Luke 9:54). They don't yet have much of a clue about the cost of discipleship, or the notion of dying to self. They are thinking out of a worldly paradigm of performance and preferment, which is why there is immediate contention and the other ten were angry with them. Jesus uses this opportunity to spell out his vision of leadership:

You know that among the Gentiles those whom they recognise as their rulers lord it over them… But it is not so among you; but whoever wishes to become great among you must be your servant, and whoever wishes to be first among you must be slave to all. For the Son of Man came not to be served but to serve, and to give his life as a ransom for many.

Mark 10:42-45

For the "practical theologians" who run Catholic schools this provides a pretty clear template about how to behave in leadership. We have to say in all honesty that this paradigm of leadership has not been practised in our schools, or indeed in the Church, for most of history, but in recent times we are coming to a new understanding. Until recently, most headteachers did not have the confidence to articulate a theology of servant leadership but there was a consistent Gospel-based view that the leadership of a Catholic school should be about service and humility:

There's always a massive risk of being seduced by ego if you're the leader. Ego-less leadership is a challenge I think for the Catholic leader – this whole obsession with what grade I am, and by extension my institution, is creating a massive egotistical culture and I don't think the Church should be subscribing to that.

Sixth Form College Principal

In a Catholic school the head kneels with the pupils, only in Catholic schools does this happen. It's lovely that because there is a greater being, there is a greater entity, isn't there? It's not that we're the God, we kneel, I kneel next to our Year 1 children and all the staff do and I think that's the sense of service, isn't it?

Preparatory School Headmaster

The advice I received from a long-serving head is that the model for you is servant leadership and he exemplified it in a rather unusual way, he said, "When you go to school, who do you think you'll find out on the front lawn picking up the litter?", and he said, "It will be me", and he said that is a form of servant leadership because you are reflecting the same way that Christ lived his life, to do whatever needed to be done, whether it meant getting your hands dirty, but not making a big exhibition of it but doing the things that even the humblest people in the school, the cleaners, are prepared to do and showing that to everybody else.

Primary School Headteacher

The washing of the feet in John's Gospel as the image *par excellence* of servant leadership has been given global prominence by the example of Pope Francis, who has washed and kissed the feet of the lost and the least in societal terms. I have enjoyed some stimulating conversations with others who are not convinced by the theological basis of regarding Jesus as a servant leader. That is not a discussion I have the competence to contribute to, but I can turn again to "The Joy of the Gospel", which has some characteristically direct comments about leadership:

Clearly Jesus does not want us to be grandees who look down upon others, but men and women of the people. This is not an idea of the Pope, or one pastoral option among others; they are injunctions contained in the word of God which are so clear, direct and convincing that they need no interpretations which might diminish their power to challenge us. Let us live them sine glossa, without commentaries. [4]

That rather exasperated "*sine glossa*" sounds almost like a rebuke to those who have spent too long theorising about things rather than just getting on with it. Our Catholic school leaders get on with things every day with great heart and they negotiate constantly between the imperatives of service and the rigorous demands of running a school. It should also be stated quite clearly that service in Christian leadership does not mean meekness; you would not last five minutes. Rather, as Francis says, it is about a learned disposition; not looking down on others, not playing the grandee, but being grounded.

For a more systematic treatment of the concept of servant leadership we have to look outside of the Church. The idea was developed by the American Robert K. Greenleaf[5] in response to autocratic approaches to leadership in the business community which were widespread in the 1970s. Greenleaf was inspired by the novel *Journey to the East* by Herman Hesse, which tells the story of a group of people on a spiritual quest. They are accompanied by Leo, a servant who sustains them with his spirit and song. He is a person of extraordinary charisma and presence. When Leo disappears one day, the group disintegrates and the journey is abandoned. Many years later the narrator discovers Leo by chance in the religious order which sponsored the original journey. He discovers that Leo is in fact the head of the order, a true leader.

Larry Spears[6] distilled Greenleaf's model for leadership into a conceptual framework with ten characteristics: listening, empathy, healing, awareness, persuasion, conceptualisation, foresight, stewardship, commitment to the growth of people, and building community. These are the means by which the ethical perspective inherent in servant leadership can be achieved. There has been a good deal of commentary on the Greenleaf/Spears model of servant leadership. It does not have a theological or empirical basis, so it should be treated with caution, but the idea is now so widespread and resonates with so many leaders that it is worth exploring in some detail and, better still, subjecting it to our own experience of leadership in Catholic schools.

Sister Mary John Mananzan presented a paper at the 2013 BENET Conference (the international Benedictine educational community) in Manila which took Spears' ten characteristics and adapted them to the Benedictine academic leader.[7] A useful exercise for any Catholic leader could be to look closely at the categories below and apply them to your own experience and the model of leadership we find in the Gospel.

Listening and Availability

As leaders we need to be not just in the room but fully attentive to whomever is in front of us. I have come across some headteachers in my career who gave me the impression that they just weren't listening. The effect of that is that you stop talking to them. What's the point? Pope Francis speaks strongly about the need for pastoral leaders to be available, not locked away in self-constructed towers of importance. Sister Mary John also emphasises the need to "pay attention to what remains unspoken" – to be finely tuned to the inner voice and nuances of communication. Daniel Goleman would consider this to be a characteristic of emotional intelligence.[8] It also means listening to everybody – giving as much of a platform to staff and parent voice as student voice.

Availability is vital to servant leadership. Another way to describe this is *presence*. All the headteachers I have ever considered to be successful had this in common: they were highly visible around the school and they made time for people. The opposite of presence I would say is not absence but *withdrawal*, and that can be so damaging for a headteacher. It is very tempting; you're tired, worn down by all the agendas, and you just want to withdraw into your office, or worse still physically withdraw on days out of school which you convince yourself are valuable. The servant leader has to be braver than that.

We have already mentioned the moment in Luke's Gospel when Jesus was looking forward to some reflective time with his disciples but the crowd had other ideas. There is an even more moving episode in Matthew's Gospel. Jesus has just been told that John the Baptist, his cousin and great mentor, had been executed by Herod. He needs to get away, he is clearly deeply grieving, but he cannot escape:

Now when Jesus heard this, he withdrew from there in a boat to a deserted place by himself. But when the crowds heard it, they followed him on foot from the towns. When he went ashore, he saw a great crowd; and he had compassion for them and cured their sick.

Matthew 14:13-14

Even in his darkest hour of grief Jesus makes himself available to the crowd because they need him and this is his mission.

Empathy

A servant leader attempts to get alongside others. This has to be a central feature of the "art of accompaniment" Francis refers to in his encyclical. When you ask headteachers what their biggest challenge is they will often say personnel issues, dealing with staff in moments of contention. It does help to try and see the situation from the perspective of the other. In the words of Sr Mary John: "administrators should not make themselves the measure of judging others but should take them as they are."[9]

Most conflict, I have come to realise, takes place inside your own head. We allow colleagues to take up residence there and act out scenes of conflict which tend to work out quite differently in reality. If we see the issue from the point of view of our colleague and pray for a wise resolution to the situation, it can prevent the escalation of the drama. There is a long tradition in the Church, going back to the desert fathers, of training thoughts before they result in the actions of sin. The same discipline would help us to place ourselves imaginatively in the place of the other, which very often allows us to see their behaviour as not irrational and certainly not personal against us.

There will be times of course when the contention goes beyond differences of opinion and personal politics. There will be times, hopefully not too many, when we are dealing with disciplinary or capability issues. The servant leader will not duck these issues but remain focused on the purpose of the school: to look after and educate children and young people in an atmosphere animated by the Gospel. If any adult undermines that purpose then the matter has to be dealt with. Perhaps the difference with the Christian servant leader is that he or she will treat the individual with consideration and compassion, without ever losing sight of the impact of the behaviour on the community.

Healing

The practice of empathy should result in more healing and reconciliation in the community. A great strength of a servant leader is the "ability for healing themselves and others"[10] to help to solve problems and resolve conflicts. The Christian leader must practise healing and reconciliation, or those grievances will grow and harden into unresolved conflict. It seems to me that this characteristic of the servant leader goes right to the heart of the Gospel. So much of the ministry of Jesus was devoted to healing. The pattern was usually spiritual healing, or forgiveness, followed by physical healing. In the cure of the paralytic (Mark 2:1-12), the man doesn't even ask for forgiveness, but gets it anyway. Jesus heals him physically to show the doubters that the Son of Man has authority to forgive sins.

Headteachers who have lost their way are often the ones who bear a grudge. The same is true of all relationships, among the students and staff, and at home. We do not always have to please people as a Catholic leader, but I believe that the Gospel calls upon us to be reconciled to our neighbour, if not always to agree. At the third national retreat for Catholic headteachers, Fr Timothy Radcliffe OP provided us with an inspiring meditation on Christian leadership based on the parable of the prodigal son. If you take the father as an exemplar of the leader, then notice how he *takes the first step* when he sees his errant son returning home. He does not have to be convinced to forgive him.

Many of us, on the other hand, may identify with the dutiful son. Once the father and returned son have been reconciled the elder son excludes himself from

the banquet (grace) because he keeps his brother, and himself, locked in a state of unforgiveness. When you hold on to righteous hurt, you do more damage to yourself. It is not always easy in school. You have convinced yourself that you are right and do not feel you should take the first step towards that vexatious colleague, but it looks as if that is what the Gospel calls us to do.

Awareness

A servant leader needs to gain general awareness and especially self-awareness. It can take a long time to come to an understanding of your own responses and emotions. We'll look in more detail at what might be our unconscious social motives in the next chapter. One headteacher I spoke to had a personal mantra from the sayings of St Bernard of Clairvaux which ran: "Notice everything. Correct little. Cherish the brethren."

We should also be on our guard against two other demons which can psychologically destroy leaders: paranoia and self-pity. Being aware of what is going on around us and within us can easily tip into paranoia and we end up believing that everybody has got it in for us, when it's probably only one or two.

Persuasion

In the words of Sr Mary John: "Servant leaders do not take advantage of their power and status by coercing compliance."[11] In the Gospels, we have perhaps the best example of this trait of servant leadership. Jesus does not always preach directly, partly because it might have been dangerous. His favourite pedagogical method is the parable, which is an invitation to challenge and change using story and simile to present the kingdom perspective. Later in this chapter we will examine the Council of Jerusalem around AD 50 as another classic example of the use of persuasion in authority.

John Sullivan, in *Catholic Schools in Contention*, identifies six priorities for Catholic school leaders. The first one is very similar to this trait: "in the use of authority, favour trust over control." He says that, "in any dispute, they [the leader] should be concerned to win people over rather than simply win."[12]

Conceptualisation

This is about seeing beyond the limits of the daily running of the community and being the one who will, again according to Sr Mary John, always, "have the vision of the school before them having made it their own vision."[13] In Chapter Three I mentioned the importance of making the school mission part of your own spirituality, and vice versa. Servant leaders are bigger-picture people. It is one of the main differences between leaders and managers: somebody has to keep the community focused on the mission and from time to time, with striking reminders, bring the attention back to the core purpose.

The second of Sullivan's priorities for Catholic leaders is to, "be vigilant with regard to the impact of alien ideologies."[14] The leader is the one who lives in the big picture and is attentive to any initiatives and ideologies which come the way of the school. He or she is the one who tests the new idea against the mission and then decides if it will help or hinder. The servant leader works as a kind of filter in this respect, or reverse prism: gathering in the multi-coloured rays of light which seek entry to the school and making of them one clear beam consistent with the mission.

Foresight

This is the ability to imagine the likely outcome of a situation. The servant leader needs to understand the community's past in order to have a better understanding of the current reality and identify possible outcomes in the future. Some leadership writers talk of the "scripts" which can dominate the thinking in an organisation. A servant leader can predict the script which will apply to different scenarios and if necessary work to change the script for a better outcome.

Stewardship

Sr Mary John points out that religious leaders, "have the task to hold their institution in trust for the greater good of the Church and of society."[15] We are only passing through, this is our shift, and the least we can do is ensure that what we hand on to our successors is in even better shape than what we inherited, for the sake of the young people we are called to serve. And it is about more than making sure that at the end of our tenure the budget is balanced, the results are a bit better, and there's been some building work. We are called to pass on the tradition, the message of the Gospel, in ways which make more sense to this community at this point in time. As St Paul said, we are, "servants of Christ and stewards of God's mysteries" (1 Corinthians 4:1). In another place St Paul refers to us as "clay jars" holding the treasure. It is not our gift but it is our responsibility to pass it on.

Commitment to the Growth of People

Servant leaders are driven by a conviction that people have intrinsic value. In the Christian setting this is a given. I would agree, therefore, with Sr Mary John when she says that leaders should, "nurture the personal, professional and spiritual growth of those under their care in a well worked out plan of in-service training."[16]

Particular attention needs to be paid by schools, school clusters and dioceses to the increasing problem of succession planning or bringing on the next generation of Catholic leaders. It will vary in different parts of the country, but in my diocese (not one of the traditional Catholic heartlands) we have seen applications for Catholic headships number in the twos and threes and in some cases none. Commitment to the growth of the next generation of Catholic leaders needs to be an absolute and urgent priority.

Building Community

For the final trait, Sr Mary John comments that the servant leader's priority is to build, "a loving, prayerful, compassionate community. In turn the community should serve the greater community, especially the poor and the oppressed."[17] In the next chapter we will use the Greek word *koinonia* to describe this kind of community and see how important it was in the early Church. But building a community, or preserving *koinonia*, requires wisdom, and is not the same as keeping everybody happy.

Sullivan calls this priority the need to "develop a strong sense of collegiality". As a former headteacher, he brings a very welcome common sense approach to this priority. He says that, "collegiality goes beyond congeniality in that it does not rest satisfied with harmonious relationships."[18] It is about getting the best out of people, developing their gifts, building a common purpose and creating a community which is animated by the Gospel.

Sullivan sees community in the widest sense in another of his priorities which is to "stay close to the Church". By this he means the Church at all levels of our experience: the local parish, the diocese and the international Church. The Catholic school as we have said is part of the saving mission of the Church and must never slip its moorings and drift off by itself. We have already highlighted the importance of being familiar with Church guidance and documents, but on behalf of schools I would also turn Sullivan's formulation around and, at the risk of impertinence, remind the Church to stay close to its schools. Many of the headteachers I spoke to said that they would welcome a new teaching document on the challenges facing Catholic schools in the twenty-first century, not least some authoritative guidance on the theology underpinning servant leadership.

Sullivan's other priorities for Catholic leaders (for those interested in following up his excellent work) are "ensure your school is outward-facing" (commitment to the common good) and the very worthwhile mantra, "Remember that it's all about the students".[19]

Greenleaf's "secular" model of servant leadership can and should be adapted, as we've seen above. We've also looked at some key moments from the Gospels which are foundational for a Catholic Christian version of servant leadership. One other concept which should be remembered in any discussions of Christian leadership is *kenosis*, or self-emptying. This is perhaps best expressed in the beautiful and very early passage from St Paul to the Philippians, which some scholars date from around AD 52, only twenty years after the death and resurrection of Jesus. This was probably a very early Christian hymn which Paul used in its entirety in his letter:

Let the same mind be in you that was in Christ Jesus, who, though he was in the form of God, did not regard equality with God as something to be exploited, but emptied himself, taking the form of a slave, being born in human likeness.

Philippians 2:5-7

The redemptive self-emptying of Jesus Christ is the model for all Christians. It runs through Church teaching and is a major theme in "The Joy of the Gospel". Pope Francis reminds us that "Life grows by being given away, and it weakens in isolation and comfort."[20] Servant leadership is a *kenosis*, based on the example of Jesus Christ. It is the understanding that it is not about me, or my status. It is about service before self.

> ## PAUSE AND REFLECT
>
> It is not easy to take on board ten traits and reflect on the extent to which they are developed within us. Why not take one of the traits and reflect on how you might grow in that area? Focus on that for a week or so, make some notes in your journal, engage a few trusted colleagues in reflective conversation.

[1] M. Stock, *Christ at the Centre* (London: Catholic Truth Society, 2012), p. 6.

[2] R. E. Brown, *The Critical Meaning of the Bible* (New Jersey: Paulist Press, 1981).

[3] D. McBride, *Where Does the Jesus Story Begin?* (Chawton: Redemptorist, 2006), p. 25.

[4] *Evangelii Gaudium*, 271.

[5] R. K. Greenleaf, *Servant Leadership: a Journey into the Nature of Legitimate Power and Greatness* (New Jersey: Paulist Press, 1977).

[6] L. Spears (ed.), *Practicing Servant Leadership: Succeeding through Trust, Bravery and Forgiveness* (San Francisco: Jossey-Bass, 2004).

[7] Sr Mary John Mananzan OSB, "Good zeal: the spirituality of Benedictine academic leaders". Paper presented at the 2013 BENET Conference (Manila, 23-26 October 2013).

[8] D. Goleman, *Working with Emotional Intelligence* (London: Bloomsbury, 1998).

[9] Mananzan, 2013.

[10] Ibid.

[11] Ibid.

[12] J. Sullivan, *Catholic Schools in Contention* (Dublin: Veritas, 2000), p. 156.

[13] Mananzan, 2013.

[14] Sullivan, 2000.

[15] Mananzan, 2013.

[16] Ibid.

[17] Ibid.

[18] Sullivan, 2000.

[19] Ibid.

[20] Fifth General Conference of the Latin American and Caribbean Bishops, cited in *Evangelii Gaudium*, 10.

CHAPTER 6

Who's in Charge? – the Problem of Authority

It has been suggested by some that servant leaders provide *direction* not *directions*. How does any understanding of servant leadership sit with the exercise of authority? In the day-to-day running of a school, one thing is certain: somebody has to make decisions. I have lost count of the number of times I have said to staff, "I've heard everybody's opinion, it is now my job to make a decision." The exercise of authority in a Catholic school will of course be informed by an understanding of service and will be animated by the example of Jesus. An absence of a sense of service may be felt in the kind of authority which lords it over people, where authority is arbitrary, unjust, whimsical, or clearly at the service of a rampant ego. "But," as Jesus said to his disciples, "it is not so among you" (Mark 10:43).

The word "authority" is used to describe Jesus a number of times in the Gospels. It is not an authority born out of the need for power over people, but out of integrity – a mission authority if you like. Early on in Mark's Gospel, when Jesus preaches at the synagogue in Capernaum, his hearers were, "astounded at his teaching, for he taught them as one having authority, and not as the scribes" (1:22). This rings true in our own experience. We probably could all think of someone who has a natural authority which arises out of a profound grasp of their subject, or their mission. We could also I'm sure think of

someone who has authority which arises out of the need to dominate others, with no real sense of depth.

It seems to me, however, that Jesus as an example of how to use authority in practice is not always helpful, in the sense that he was not an organisational figure. There is little evidence that part of his mission was to systematically build a community, or a Church for that matter (Jesus mentions Church only twice, in Matthew's Gospel). Jesus' mode of operation was to take the news of God's reign to a community, show them by his healing words and deeds what that looked like, and then move on to the next place. There is no evidence of him writing anything down or working out a blueprint with the Apostles. He is not a foundational figure in that sense. It should be stressed that this is not the only view of the mission intentions of Jesus. Raymond E. Brown, in *The Critical Meaning of the Bible*, describes a "rightist view", whereby Jesus foresaw the future in detail and did have a precise ecclesiastical plan. I am temperamentally inclined to what Brown calls the "centrist view" which is that Jesus had no such future knowledge:

He left behind the disciples whom he had called; to them both in his ministry and after the resurrection he gave a mission to proclaim the kingdom; he also

gave them a Spirit. Under the influence of that Spirit, as they encountered problems, they developed responses (e.g. in terms of deciding to convert Gentiles and of structuring the Church).[1]

I would like to look briefly at one example of what Brown refers to here as the early Church developing a response to an issue where they seemed to have no clear directive from Jesus to guide them. At the Council of Jerusalem, around AD 50, the early Church had one of its first major decisions to make: Could Gentiles become followers of Jesus without being circumcised according to the Law of Moses? Chapter 15 of the Acts of the Apostles describes how the major figures of the time lined up on either side of the argument. It is interesting to note that it is James, the brother of Jesus, who is in charge of the Jerusalem church, not Peter. In fact, according to Church historians the family of Jesus ran the church in Palestine until well into the second century, because they saw succession in terms of lineage, since Jesus was of the royal house of David. The arguments for both sides are delivered. The believers who are Pharisees argue for circumcision. Peter argues that this is a "yoke" which the disciples should not be asked to bear.

It is interesting to note that nobody quotes Jesus, which would presumably have ended the argument there and then, but he appears not to have said anything about this issue. So the early Church has to work this out, under the influence of the Spirit. When it comes to decision time it is James who stands up and says: "Therefore I have reached the decision that we should not trouble those Gentiles who are turning to God" (Acts 15:19). James' decision comes after a reasoned and persuasive argument (see: ten traits of servant leadership in Chapter Five) based on a close reading of the Hebrew scriptures. This is no arbitrary show of power but authority based on wisdom following an open discussion in which all sides have had their say. But in the end somebody has to make a decision. Servant leadership should never be confused with an inability to make decisions. The Church has a tradition, from the very beginning, of ecclesial decision-making which can act as a blueprint for Catholic leaders in all settings. It is quite appropriate for one person to make a decision. How that can be done is exemplified at the very first Council of the Church, almost two thousand years ago.

The understanding of authority in the early Church is further developed in John's Gospel, which was written after the Acts of the Apostles, probably towards the end of the first century. A fascinating study in this Gospel is to compare the figures of Peter and the Beloved Disciple. If we take Peter as having a primacy of authority (if not in Jerusalem, then certainly among the Apostles and in the wider

community), and the Beloved Disciple as having a primacy of love, the evangelist seems to be directing us towards some interesting conclusions.

For a full exploration of this theme I would recommend Raymond E. Brown's *The Churches the Apostles Left Behind* (Chapter Six), but in brief the disciple is consistently portrayed as more loving than Peter. At the last supper, Peter has to ask the Beloved Disciple, who is reclining on the breast of Jesus, what is going on. The Beloved Disciple is the only male disciple present at the foot of the cross and, after the race to the empty tomb between Peter and the Beloved Disciple, it is the latter who is the first to believe. When Jesus does confer upon Peter the role of shepherd of the sheep (John 21:15-17) it is only after he declares (three times – as he is allowed to redeem his denial) that he loves Jesus. Authority must be based on love – this is the message for all Christian leaders. Raymond E. Brown concludes that:

While a real person, the Beloved Disciple functions in the gospel as the embodiment of Johannine idealism: All Christians are disciples and among them greatness is determined by a loving relationship to Jesus, not by function or office. [2]

An interesting footnote to the Council of Jerusalem, when Peter again seems to be found wanting, is found in Paul's Letter to the Galatians. After the Council of Jerusalem, Peter comes to Antioch, where Paul has also returned. Peter is happy to eat with the uncircumcised, which traditional Jews would not have accepted since it would have made them unclean. However, he stops doing this when some men from "the circumcision faction" (Galatians 2:12) turn up. It seems that not all the issues were resolved in Jerusalem. The matter of the food laws, and who was allowed to eat what with whom, is clearly one of them. Those who had argued for circumcision for new Christians would also want to retain the integrity of Jewish food laws. Paul is furious at what he sees as Peter's moral weakness and he "opposed him to his face" (2:11). He is scathing about "those who were supposed to be acknowledged leaders" of the Jerusalem Church (2:6). The point is that even when a decision has been made, it might not be the whole decision and those who "lost" will keep picking away at the matter looking for little victories.

Paul is a whole other study in leadership, which is, sadly, beyond the scope of this book. His only authority comes from his personal experience of the risen Christ. That is all he needs and it is enough for him to call himself an Apostle and for him to stand up to the official authorities in the Church. We probably all have a Paul in the staffroom: passionate, committed, awkward, driven by an agenda which arises from personal conviction and more than happy to oppose leadership to its face. You won't always win with Paul and you don't have to. You can always try taking the first step.

Jorge Bergoglio – a Journey in Leadership

We have referred a great deal to the writings of Pope Francis in this study, but his life is also instructive for those reflecting on leadership in the Church. Paul Vallely, the journalist and activist on international development, traces the leadership journey of Jorge Bergoglio from a young conservative to an older servant leader in his excellent book, *Pope Francis: Untying the Knots*. At the age of only thirty-six, Bergoglio was appointed as the provincial of the Jesuits of Argentina, the same year in which he took his final Jesuit vows. Anyone who feels leadership thrust upon them at a young age will find this aspect of the story very helpful. Bergoglio was seen as a key figure in the resistance movement to the reforms of Vatican II. In the Jesuit seminary, he reintroduced old-style clerical dress, a fixed daily routine, and limited the curriculum to a traditional core.

He was very keen that the students should not become overly academic, however, and insisted that they spent their weekends tending to the needs of the poor in the most disadvantaged areas, provided they did not become involved in politics. The Bergoglio of the time was criticised for having a sentimental view of the poor and of being more interested in alleviating the symptoms of poverty rather than addressing the structural reasons for its existence. In terms of his leadership style, Vallely quotes a student from the time who preferred to remain anonymous: "I never found Bergoglio a control freak. As Provincial it was just about authority not control." He was widely regarded as dynamic, spiritual and humble, but his charismatic style had its own problems:

"If you liked him and he liked you, you'd be in a good position," recalled Rafael Velasco. "But if he didn't like you, you were in for some kind of trouble. And if you didn't agree with him you'd be relegated outside the circle of power."[3]

There is something very human and reassuring about that portrait of the man who was to go on to become the first ever Pope from South America. It is a temptation we all face. As mentioned above, Jesus himself had an inner circle. It is also very human to like some people and not like others. The challenge for leadership, and for Christian leaders especially, is not to let that show, to consciously work at being impartial and never leave yourself open to accusations of favouritism, which is corrosive.

Vallely goes on to cover the controversial topic of Bergoglio's role in the so-called "Dirty War" during the dictatorship in Argentina from 1973-1983, with particular attention to the arrest and torture of two Jesuits in his province. Vallely's treatment is meticulous and balanced and neither exonerates nor condemns the current Pope. It was a time of great darkness and if one honestly asks oneself the question *What would I have done?* it seems easier to arrive at a non-judgemental position.

The charismatic but divisive Jesuit leader is then sent off as an ordinary priest into a kind of exile in Cordoba in the late 1980s. When he is surprisingly brought back to Buenos Aires as an auxiliary bishop in 1992, he has already started on the transformational journey which will lead to the washing of the feet in the Casa del Marmo juvenile prison on Holy Thursday 2013. Vallely provides a vivid description of this seminal moment:

On his knees on the stone floor the 76-year-old Pope, vested like a deacon, washed feet which were black, white, male, female, tattooed and untattooed, and then kissed each one. The owners of the feet were Catholic, Orthodox Christians, Muslims and atheists. And two of them were women. No pope had ever washed the feet of a woman before.[4]

The rubric for the washing of feet says "viri" – men. This caused liturgists some anxiety. When Vallely asked a senior member of the Curia for his response to this breach of the rules, "he could see which way the papal wind was blowing and said, 'The Pope does not break the rules… he just remakes them.'"[5]

Bergoglio clearly came back from his exile in Cordoba a changed leader. Vallely concludes that in the long hours of prayerful exile he developed no less than a new model of leadership, "one which involved consultation, participation, collegiality and listening."[6] There are still many in Argentina and in the Jesuit order who are unconvinced by the personal style of the Jesuit Pope. What is humility, after all? Is it something we are born with or not? If so, then what chance do those born without it have of being servant leaders? If not, can it be learned? If it is a natural disposition, then it seems rather deterministic: you will be humble whether you like it or not. But Vallely's treatment of the Bergoglio story comes to the view that humility is a virtue the current Bishop of Rome has learned because it is how he should behave as a servant of the servants of God:

Bergoglio's humility was not some natural modesty, bashfulness or self-effacement. It was certainly far from the same thing as meekness. In Pope Francis humility is an intellectual stance and a religious decision. It is a virtue which his will must seek to impose on a personality which has its share of pride and a propensity to dogmatic and domineering behaviour. Humility is a consciousness which wrestles against the unconsciousness of the human ego. [7]

That passage is well worth reflecting on in some depth. We all have our default settings, the way we naturally respond when we are crossed or demeaned. What Bergoglio's journey teaches us, in much the same way as the Gospels, is that Christian leadership is a journey of self-emptying, and it takes years; slowly but surely dismantling our own ego, our need for control and achievement, for the sake of a grace-filled response to the community in front of us. This in fact may serve as a description of the journey the Church herself has been on in recent years.

Strong Leadership?

To bring us back to the school setting, it cannot be stressed enough that Christian leadership, or servant leadership, has nothing to do with meekness or false humility. There will be times when the community needs strong leadership and authority. Some of our school leaders will find themselves in very trying circumstances. The school may be in an Ofsted category and the scale of the challenge may be overwhelming. Even if the school is not officially in trouble, some school settings require very robust leadership because of the catchment area or profile of the staff.

Gerald Grace considers this issue and the unhelpful media stereotype of the leader who will rescue the situation:

dominant, executive school leaders… who would be able to "turn around" a difficult school by personal dynamism, competitive skill and market intelligence and by the ability to give strong leadership and to take tough decisions. [8]

What is the Catholic version of this kind of leadership? In fact, there is very little in any of the thinking outlined above which would prevent a Catholic leader coming into a challenging situation and making a difference. As I said in the chapters on mission thinking, the situation of the school needs to be understood first and then the mission priorities established. A clear focus on the dignity and needs of the pupils or students, especially the vulnerable, will provide the school leader with all the moral purpose necessary for the job in hand.

The macho head or "super-head" no longer has much credibility in the wider educational community. It is not just in servant leadership where you will find convergence between Church thinking and secular models. In a very well-known and respected research project in the commercial sector, the American Jim Collins set out to answer the question, "Can a good company become a great company and if so how?" The portrait of the leader who can deliver the "good to great" journey was surprising and has much relevance for schools. Having studied the success trajectories of almost fifteen hundred *Fortune 500* companies, Collins and his team found a remarkable degree of agreement regarding the qualities of leadership which consistently delivered sustainable success. Yes, the charismatic leaders had immediate and dramatic impact, but when they left the companies often went into decline, since there was no leadership in place to sustain growth. They found five ascending levels of leadership characteristics, all of which were needed for success. But the Level Five leader, the one who consistently achieved and sustained greatness in all the companies analysed in the research, had two very compelling characteristics: *humility* and *will*. Collins defined the most effective leadership as follows:

Level 5 leaders channel their ego needs away from themselves and into the larger goal of building a great company. It's not that Level 5 leaders have no ego or self-interest. Indeed they are incredibly ambitious – but their ambition is first and foremost for the institution, not themselves.[9]

Collins stresses the fact that his conclusions are empirical and not ideological. It is the other way round for Catholic leaders, but nevertheless fascinating, and reassuring, that the Gospel path of

"ego-less" leadership will also result in good outcomes. But then we already knew that from our own experience and all the available data. If we look in the New Testament we also find the other trait of Collins' Level Five leadership in abundance: *will*. The number of miles covered by the early preachers, especially Paul, was quite remarkable. They were not building a *Fortune 500* company but their application of humility and will allowed the Good News of the Gospel to spread to the furthest ends of the Roman Empire.

Leading a Community

In this chapter we have looked to scripture for models of Christian leadership and it is there we should look for a description of the Christian community the servant leader is expected to lead. Schools are not Christian communities in the same way that the early communities of the Church were Christian. Our school communities have colleagues and pupils who are not Christian, but we are part of the wider community of the Church and should look to the exemplary models of the Church for guidance. In Acts, Luke provides us with a portrait of the early community and what defined them: "They devoted themselves to the apostles' teaching and fellowship, to the breaking of bread and the prayers" (2:42).

This is what defined them as a community and it could well serve as a useful reminder for what should be evident in our Catholic schools (for more systematic thinking based on the structures of the early Church, see the 5W framework in the sibling book by Sister Judith Russi). Our main purpose is to be faithful to the teaching of the Apostles in ways our young people understand, through our religious education programme, our assemblies and liturgies. We are called to be Eucharistic communities, which break bread together and celebrate the Mass in ways which engage a young modern audience without compromising on the tradition and mystery of what is being celebrated. In all of this we are called to act in fellowship with one another. In the last chapter we touched upon this concept of *koinonia*, and how it should not be confused with a superficial attention to harmony. The notion has always been of central importance to the Church and has come to the fore again in recent years. In *The Spirituality of Leadership*, Fr James Hanvey SJ draws attention to fellowship as one of the main characteristics of a spirituality of leadership. He defines it thus:

Koinonia implies a new way of thinking, working and relating. It can recognise giftedness – not just the gifts that are normally identified within our current educational orthodoxy, but the gifts that come to light and have a right to be nourished when we look at a person with graced eyes and see them within the perspective of eternity.[10]

Those "graced eyes" remind us of the call of Pope Francis to see the "sacred grandeur" in our brothers and sisters, and the invitation to recognise giftedness takes us back to what "New Vocations" called the "original gift" in every person (for more see Chapters One and Two). *Koinonia* invites us to live in a community in which the members see each other in the light of Christian revelation. It invites us to see their gifts and help them to flourish as children of God. The New Testament is full of examples of how this fellowship should be experienced in the daily life of community. St Paul, writing to the Galatians, encourages them to, "Bear one another's burdens" (6:2) and in his First Letter to the Corinthians we have the great catalogue of gifts which individual members bring to the community as a gift for each other (1 Corinthians 12:1-11). The fellowship will be tested and at times in the history of the Church it has been tested to breaking point, but at the Council of Jerusalem we saw an example of how the fellowship was preserved, and running through our reflections have been insights into how to run a community to ensure that *koinonia* is a living reality.

The final aspect of Luke's defining characteristics of the early community is "the prayers". Raymond E. Brown comments that many of the very earliest Christian prayers were probably fragments taken from the Hebrew scriptures (and can be found in

Luke's Gospel, for example the words of Mary's *Magnificat* or Simeon's *Nunc Dimittis* in the Temple). They would then have composed their own prayers, as we saw in the last chapter, in the example from St Paul's Letter to the Philippians. We have been composing prayers ever since. According to the *Youth Catechism*, there are five main types of prayer: blessing and adoration; prayer of petition; prayer of intercession; prayer of thanksgiving; and prayer of praise. It may seem an obvious point but it struck me very forcibly when I visited sixteen Catholic schools in a short space of time, that one of the very strongly defining characteristics of our schools is that *we pray*. It is also remarkable how something so profoundly counter-cultural is so normative an experience for our students:

Before Mass, we always prepare some prayers and write it down and put them in a basket at the front and sometimes Miss reads them all and she picks one that she thought really stood out to her and if they want to they get to read their own prayer in the Mass.

Year 5 Pupil

We have morning prayer. If you have a tutor lesson then our teacher will have a prayer book. In every tutor room there's a prayer book with a thousand prayers. It's a really nice book with modern prayers and we will read a few prayers and say the Our Father. And in assemblies we always say the Our Father.

Year 8 Student

Before every lesson we start with a prayer and we have two assemblies a week, house assembly which is led by the headteacher who reads the Gospel and we say prayers, and year assembly when we say prayers.

Year 10 Student

The commitment to the prayer life of our students means that they will leave our schools with very powerful memories of praying as a community and in the silence of their hearts. For a generation which we regard as the most removed from the tradition of the Church this is so important. One former headteacher described to me a Year Eleven leavers' liturgy which I'm sure will live in the memory of the students for a very long time:

I had a chaplain who designed the end of Year 11 Mass which I thought was one of the most moving experiences of witness to the faith in the school. Every single boy, a hundred and ninety boys, put a candle on the altar, their own candle, and they were given the time, each of them, to have a few moments of reflection and every single boy in that school felt as if they were part of something bigger. When the whole altar was lit up and flickering with candles it was very powerful.

Former Secondary Headteacher, still in Catholic education

In the next chapter we will look a little into the theology of prayer, but it is very important that our children and young people understand the importance of the different types of prayer, of speaking out loud to God. We do not assume that we change the mind of God when we pray, but we wish to change our mind, our hearts, and become more attentive to the needs of our brothers and sisters, the needs of our world, more humble and thankful before the loving mystery of God.

The Catholic headteacher is expected to lead the school in prayer. Whether we see ourselves as servant leaders, faith leaders, Christian leaders, or under any other heading, we will not be able to do that unless we are on a genuine journey of discipleship. According to Hanvey it is the number one characteristic of spiritual leadership: "Although obvious, it bears underlining that there can be no spiritual leadership if we do not nourish our relationship with Christ and the Spirit."[11] As Catholic leaders we overlap with our colleagues in non-faith settings in very many respects, but unless we have a personal faith, or are on a journey of prayerful transformation ourselves, we will be paying mere lip service to the mission.

PAUSE AND REFLECT

- How do we exercise authority in our leadership role in school?
- To what extent are the characteristics of a Christian community identified in the Acts of the Apostles (the Apostles' teaching, breaking of the bread, community and prayers) evident in our school community?

[1] R. E. Brown, *The Critical Meaning of the Bible* (New Jersey: Paulist Press, 1981), p. 92.
[2] R. E. Brown, *The Churches the Apostles Left Behind* (New Jersey: Paulist Press, 1984), p. 93.
[3] P. Vallely, *Pope Francis: Untying the Knots* (London: Bloomsbury, 2013), p. 51.
[4] Ibid., p. 187.
[5] Ibid., p. 187.
[6] Ibid., p. 194.
[7] Ibid., p. 196.
[8] G. Grace, *Catholic Schools: Mission, Markets and Morality* (Abingdon: Routledge Falmer, 2002), p. 143.
[9] J. Collins, *Good to Great* (London: Random House, 2001), p. 21.
[10] J. Hanvey SJ, *The Spirituality of Leadership* (London: Heythrop Institute for Religion, Ethics and Public Life, 2008), p. 25.
[11] Ibid., p. 24.

CHAPTER 7

How to Survive and Thrive in Catholic Leadership

You can have all the best mission insights going and the most profound understanding of servant leadership, but if you don't have an actual person who can cope with the demands of being that type of leader, it really won't make any difference. The human being who is called upon to lead today's Catholic school is under more pressure than ever before. It is *intense*. One colleague pointed out to me that most headteachers have dealt with more issues before 8 a.m. than most leaders in other professions. It's true. First thing in the morning is a time for people to "catch you" before the teaching day begins and for parents to see you before they have to go to work. One headteacher I interviewed told me he was in work every day by 6 a.m. I discovered later that this wasn't entirely accurate. When I emailed him to say thanks for a wonderful visit to his school, he replied at 5.53 a.m.! Long days, constant pressure, high expectations – how do we ensure that our leaders not only survive, but thrive in this demanding environment?

This chapter will explore some ideas for how Catholic heads can not only cope with the role but bring vibrant mission leadership to the communities they serve. There is no shortage of wisdom from the wider academic community about how this can be achieved. A full review of the literature is not the purpose of this book, but one writer on leadership I have found consistently helpful over the years is Michael Fullan, currently Professor Emeritus of the Ontario Institute for Studies in Education of the University of Toronto. He is widely recognised as an international authority on educational reform and has written many books, but the one which has had the biggest influence on me is *Leading in a Culture of Change*. It is very readable, intelligent and intuitive. It is also very much to the point: we are leading in a culture of almost constant change, driven not only by the national political agenda but also the wider developments in society. In his search for the secret of surviving and thriving in leadership in a culture of change Fullan discovered "a set of seemingly more personal characteristics that all effective leaders possess… the energy-enthusiasm-hopefulness constellation."[1]

In this course of my research, I visited sixteen schools – primary, secondary, post-sixteen, maintained and independent – and it was remarkable to note that all of the headteachers who showed me round their school communities had that "constellation" of energy, enthusiasm and hope. First impressions make a huge difference when you visit a school: your first sight of the students as you arrive, the reception area (Where's the mission statement?), the receptionist (How long does it take them to notice you're there?) and then, after a few minutes of flicking through the press cuttings on the comfy chairs, the headteacher: "Good morning, welcome, great to see you."

Within the first few seconds you form an impression of this person and if you sense energy, enthusiasm and hope embodied in a smile, good eye contact and a handshake, you feel you have met a leader who wants to be where they are, is not weighed down by expectation, and has the attributes to lead this school with confidence. It is of course only the tip of the iceberg, but if the headteacher then shows you around the school, within thirty minutes you have a very good understanding of the leader you are dealing with: what they choose to point out, how they walk into a classroom, the relationship with students and staff, even the pace and purpose with which they walk around the site; it is remarkably revealing. Bear that in mind the next time the inspector calls, or any other visitor for that matter.

You can't lead any school, let alone a Catholic school, without energy; it's another one for the *sine qua non* list. It's not easy, of course, if like me you were not born a natural athlete. We all know colleagues I'm sure who seem to have enviable reserves of stamina which allow them to pop up at morning briefings after the most gruelling week looking as fresh as the proverbial daisy. But for the rest of us it's a slog and something we have to work on with conscious attention to diet, exercise and a sensible diary. We also have to develop an understanding of what gives us energy and what takes it away. In the next chapter I will look more closely at why we might gravitate to certain types of activity which we find energy givers. We can also help ourselves by establishing some framework for conversations with staff. One of my

mantras over the years has been: I don't want to hear the problem (moaning is an energy drainer) but I want to hear the solution (which is often an energy giver). And also remember that energy on its own is no guarantee of effectiveness; it must be channelled according to the vision and priorities of the school. Energy without direction will wear people out very quickly. Nobody wants to be led by a headless chicken.

Enthusiasm is also a must. You just can't imagine an effective headteacher who is not enthusiastic about the school and the plan for improvement, although we may all know some colleagues who have sadly lost that enthusiasm over the years. I learned all over again the importance of enthusiasm in a spell of executive leadership, when I was asked to lead a smaller, more fragile school as well as my own. Staff morale was low and the school had been told for too long that it was in line for closure. I also discovered that technology had put an end to Monday morning briefings – it could all be done so much more efficiently online. That was set up for a nice early win. I brought back Monday morning briefings, which got all the staff together in one room. I knew from my experience of other schools that no matter how I felt I had to at least look and sound enthusiastic, and I very often convinced myself: a prayer, positive messages, notices for the week, have a good day!

It did make a difference and was very welcome by the staff, as was the Friday morning briefing when we basically thanked staff for all the good work they had done. Of course there's no point in having a great morning briefing and then spending the rest of the day in your office. The message was reinforced by walks around the school, which the staff liked and which I always found gave me energy and enthusiasm rather than taking it away. I have never been able to manage a daily walk around school but I believe that it should be on any headteacher's list of good habits.

The final essential element of our constellation is hope, or as I have seen it described in some leadership tracts, "unwarranted optimism". I do often wonder what the foundation for that hope or optimism is in secular thinking? It seems to me it can only be a kind of natural disposition, which doesn't help those who are naturally pessimistic. Maybe they just shouldn't be headteachers. In the Christian tradition hope has an objective foundation. It is one of the three "supernatural" virtues, along with faith and love, and will "abide", according to St Paul in his great letter to the Corinthians. Hope is defined in the *Youth Catechism of the Catholic Church* (a recommendation for Catholics of all ages) as:

trusting in what God has promised us in creation, in the prophets, but especially in Jesus Christ, even though we do not yet see it. God's Holy Spirit is given to us so that we can patiently hope for the Truth.[2]

The Christian story always ends with hope. If the two disciples had reached Emmaus without the stranger appearing by their side they would have gone on to live quietly disappointed lives. If our last image of Jesus was of him collapsed in the garden or being taken limply down from the cross then we would have lost interest a long time ago. But our story ends with resurrection, Pentecost and mission, and that is one of the reasons for the hope that is in us.

Sustaining energy, enthusiasm and hope in our leaders is vital, because one thing is for sure – the challenges we face are daunting, growing in complexity, and coming at us from all directions. We have the pressures of a political agenda which demands that we perform ever more effectively, often with a very narrow matrix of performance. We have the pressures of accountability and inspection. The bar keeps being nudged up and headteachers increasingly feel more like football managers: one bad result away from the sack. We face the challenge of the bewildering growth of the digital network which has created a divide between digital natives and digital immigrants (I'm not convinced it's entirely about what age you are, but that's part of it), and has given young people the opportunities for self-projection which they sometimes get badly wrong. We also have the constant pressure as Christian leaders of operating in a society in which the language and presence of religion are rapidly being consigned to a historical curiosity and the worship of the "golden calves" of material gain and physical perfection (as narrowly defined by the industries who benefit) is predominant. We are challenged by the increase in our young people of behavioural disorders and mental health problems.

Some people call this "chaos" and some academics have made a career out of it. It probably wouldn't do much for our psychological equilibrium if we read too much about chaos theory, but Fullan is a sensible guide through the more dramatic outcrops of that thinking. He quotes a striking line from G. K. Chesterton which has been taken up by chaos theorists: "wildness lies in wait". We hope there's not too much wildness waiting for us in school on a

Monday morning but the point is understood by hearing from Chesterton, a writer with a profoundly Catholic vision of humanity, at greater length:

The real trouble with this world of ours is not that it is an unreasonable world, or even that it is a reasonable one. The commonest kind of trouble is that it is nearly reasonable, but not quite. Life is not an illogicality; yet it is a trap for logicians. It looks just a little more mathematical and regular than it is; its exactitude is obvious, but its inexactitude is hidden; its wildness lies in wait.[3]

Christian leaders have an instinctive understanding of the human condition as blessed, but broken, not entirely reasonable. We are not surprised by "inexactitude" and we know that "wildness" is sometimes just under the surface and we do our utmost to prevent its eruption. One of our greatest temptations as leaders is to tidy up, to separate the darnel from the wheat before the harvest, whether that means removing a disruptive child or a recalcitrant colleague. The daily reality of leadership is more often about dealing with crisis and complexity. I well remember the blissful days when I was a head of department. I worked long hours, the marking load was very heavy (as all English teachers will tell you) but my days were largely *predictable*. I more or less knew what issues I would have with which colleagues, which students might cause a little difficulty, and which parents might be on the phone looking for more homework for their gifted child.

The daily experience of headship is not knowing what's waiting for you when you walk in the door and knowing that most of what you will have to face is not covered in the manual. You need to embrace complexity and crisis. It doesn't mean that every day is a crisis, but when there is one, everybody looks to you to lead the response. I am very attracted by the prospect of achieving an Eden-like state of perfection, but that's not likely to happen in any community. Also, in the parable of the wheat and darnel (Matthew 13:24-30) Jesus warns us against over-zealous gardening. To cope with such demands means developing certain qualities, among them, of course, resilience, but also a certain gift for improvisation, flexibility, the need to be light on your feet and not doggedly committed to any one way of doing things. There will be times however when no amount of nifty footwork will preserve you from the body blows.

Leadership goes in cycles, depending on how long you have been in your school and what circumstances prevail. I have experienced several cycles of intense pressure in headship, either because of managing major change, managing the need for rapid improvement, or managing critical incidents. Those times can be a trial, a kind of personal Gethsemane, when you feel you are on the floor. I vividly remember the personal cost of those periods of intensity. When our sons were younger there were some weeks when I would be out of the house before they woke up and home when they were asleep. I would be too tired sometimes to even *speak* to my wife. It wasn't good, it wasn't healthy and it wasn't sustainable. All of the headteachers I spoke to admitted to very trying times, when they were taken to the very edge of their resources:

I've had to deal with some of the most serious things you can do as a headteacher, whether it's telling a student that their father has tragically died or dealing with a family whose child's been murdered. What you bring to those occasions is, well there's no manual for it, but what you do bring to it is the cura personalis [care of the person or individual, a Jesuit principle] that you're on this journey with them.

Former Secondary Headteacher, still in Catholic education

I think dealing with people, adults who are suffering because they've reached a stage where they cannot come up to the standards that are expected, for whatever reason, is the biggest challenge. I think that's really hard because there's a part of you that compassionately wants to just say, "It'll be fine," and there's another part saying, "I can't say that, I've got to see this through." I've had to get rid of probably about twenty staff since I arrived, one way or another, either encouraged or paid or told and with some of them it's been genuinely very, very difficult to do that. That's very, very tough.

Secondary Headteacher

Governors have a critical role here, in fact a *duty*, to look after their headteacher and to ensure they are having conversations with him or her about how they are coping with the challenges of change and crisis. I managed to stay on my feet through those difficult times, more through luck than judgement, but I know too many colleagues who have not. It is a human tragedy when colleagues crack and crumble. I have now seen that happen too many times. The care of headteachers must be a priority. The governing body,

should have a memorandum of some kind in place to determine the expectations of the head in terms of working time and attendance at meetings, otherwise there is no chance of that necessary constellation of energy-enthusiasm-hope being sustained. In one case I know a governing body put a memorandum in place when the headteacher came back after a long illness. Better late than never, I suppose, but even better if it had been there from the beginning.

I asked all the headteachers I visited how they coped with the pressure; did they have a work/life balance? The question was often greeted with a wry smile. One headteacher simply said:

It's gone. It's gradually got worse and worse. We've been working and fighting to improve and keep our numbers up throughout the recession and people have got more discerning and want more for their buck. We're monitoring more, trying to improve performance, doing a lot more around teaching and learning than maybe I did five years ago. It's a bit of a worry to be honest.

Preparatory School Headmaster

A long-serving primary headteacher who was about to retire at fifty-five, prompted largely by the lack of work/life balance in his life, commented:

I'm also very lucky in that the people that love me personally are tremendously generous in how little they see of me. I'm not going to make any bones about the fact that there's a significant element in the decision that I've made to retire is about making

a bit of a change in my life. I don't expect to be
sitting around at home but I would like to climb
down from some of the hours I do now because, well
it's rude actually, apart from anything else and I
don't like rudeness.

Primary School Headteacher

There were one or two who seemed to have
achieved a happy balance. One secondary
headteacher was prepared to have long, full-on days
but took little work home and managed to protect his
weekends. I told him he needed to write the book
about how to do that and retire. For most it is a
struggle, but good use of time and determined effort
not to let work consume every second is the key:

You do need other things in your life to be a better
leader it seems to me. I hate it if I go for a week
without being in the gym three or four times. I love
my telly, I try to read at least fifteen books a year
and I write notes on every book I read.

Sixth Form College Principal

Leadership does involve heavy lifting and that means
long hours at times, but a good governing body will
monitor that and make sure the hours don't take their
toll. Pressure comes with the job. I don't think
pressure can be avoided but it's when pressure
becomes *stress* (that is to say you experience an
adverse physical and mental reaction because of the
pressure) that you are potentially in trouble. Stress is
what must be avoided or minimised as much as
possible. In schools we still have a very generous
holiday allocation compared to the rest of the public
and commercial sector, and while much of it is taken

up with work at least it feels a bit like "downtime"
when the car park is empty and the pressure lets go
of you to some extent. Then there is the wisdom
which our faith brings to this issue. The Christian
tradition, and indeed the Jewish tradition, has always
insisted on Sabbath, and that is a concept that we
would do well to revive and encourage among our
leaders. It seems a blindingly obvious point: take
Sunday off, go to church, eat with your family, take
the dog for a walk, look at the sky, but I can hear the
heads say yes, but I just need to check my emails…

The authors of *On the Way to Life* provide us with a
number of valuable insights into contemporary
culture. One of the features they describe is the
distortion of time, or more dramatically the theft of
time we experience as citizens of the modern age.
Technology was supposed to convert more of our
time to leisure time but it doesn't feel that way: there
seems less time than there used to be. The icon of
this troubling development in our culture is the
mobile phone, which now seems to be ubiquitous.
Our surveys in school tell us that by the time the
students are fourteen years old, mobile phone
possession has risen to around ninety per cent. It has
very quickly come to be perceived as a necessity of
modern life, despite the dangers:

The irony is that this very symbol of in-touchness
only serves to show the poverty of our
communication and loss of our private space. The
boundaries between office and home are erased, our
public and private selves merge… However, it
means that "our" time is constantly colonised by
work so that we become "willing slaves".[4]

One headteacher I spoke to complained about the impact of emails, which he could access on his phone. He learned the hard way once after he checked his emails just before bed-time only to discover a little "bomb" from a member of staff in the inbox. It detonated in the middle of the night, in his head. His private space was trashed. Now he doesn't look at emails after 7 p.m., reasoning that first thing in the morning he's more able to deal with whatever lies in wait. As headteachers, and especially as Catholic headteachers, we owe it to ourselves, our nearest and dearest and our communities, to steal back time. This is not just for the sake of spiritual health, but for the sake of being a better leader.

Michael Fullan argues that to lead effectively on the edge of chaos (or if you prefer, in a culture of change) we need "slow thinking". This concept is not unfamiliar to the Catholic tradition; we call it *reflection*, the time needed to absorb what is going on around us and arrive at a course of action that resembles wisdom. In the Ignatian prayer tradition it is the *examen*, the review of the day's events looking for the promptings of the Spirit in our encounters. In a culture where speed of response and speed of thinking seems to be increasing at an unhealthy rate, we must apply the brakes and make time for reflection. The African poet Ben Okri expresses this idea beautifully in "To an English Friend in Africa" –

Live slowly, think slowly, for time is a mystery.
Never forget that love
Requires you to be
The greatest person you are capable of being,
Self-generating and strong and gentle.[5]

Time is a mystery; to the Christian mind, it is a sacred mystery. We do give a lot of attention in our schools to creating sacred *space*, on the assumption that today's distracted children need a place they can walk into and experience a different atmosphere. The running water, incense and tranquil music are important and we do need spaces like that, but that's not what Jesus said to the woman he met at the well. He told her that the time had arrived when the place was not what mattered but worshipping in spirit and in truth. When you stop thinking about sacred space you focus instead on *sacred time*. That, I believe, is a more effective way to combat the theft of time which is such a chronic problem in our working lives. Sacred time can happen anywhere. Richard Rohr calls sacred time our constant contact with eternity which is available to us whenever we want. Modern culture lives on the surface and that is not the best place to find God. Our God is subtle, some would say shy. The Christian life invites us into depth and stillness to encounter that God, to put out into the deep. In the previous chapter we observed that our schools pray. In order to pray we need to create the time more than the space. Sacred time is an invitation to prayerful encounter with God. It only requires us to call it so; mark it with the sign of the cross. It can happen anywhere you like; by a well, by the shore of a lake, in a classroom.

Slow thinking, reflection, *examen*, are all critical in our battle against the thieves of time and our ability to cope with pressure. The other aspect of thinking which is helpful for effective leadership is *best thinking*. I can't source whose idea this is, it was one of those occasions when the phrase stays with you but who said it and when has slipped away. At any rate, somewhere in my professional journey somebody defined highly effective leadership as *giving to other people your best thinking*. That formulation has helped me a great deal. Hence, one of my key questions at the beginning of the week or term is: Which colleague, meeting or event this week, this term, requires my best thinking?

There is also a very important communal aspect to this. We can get so far thinking alone, but I have always enjoyed the creativity of group thinking and discussion. Allowing time for that in and out of school will keep the project fresh and keep you motivated. It should also help to reduce stress. If you are well prepared and somewhat ahead of yourself then you're less likely to experience stress. It also shows a great deal of respect for what you're doing. This project, this person, this team, deserves my very best thinking and that is what I will bring to the table.

Tim Brighouse, a former Chief Education Officer and Schools Commissioner for London and another of those educationalists it's always worth listening to, produced a very sensible and helpful pamphlet a few years ago called *How Successful Head Teachers Survive and Thrive*. He examines work/life balance and, while reminding us that headteachers have to work hard, he concedes the need for balance and uses some memorable lines of poetry to make the point. They are provided by Alec Clegg, a former Chief Education Officer of West Riding. As a teenager, Clegg would visit his aunt in Grantham (birthplace of Margaret Thatcher, perhaps not the best role model for work/life balance) and was always struck by a neatly stitched sampler on the wall which read:

If of fortune thou be bereft
And of thine earthly store have left
Two loaves, sell one and with the dole
Buy hyacinths to feed the soul.[6]

Good advice for any leader, especially those whose very identity as leaders is nourished by the soul, or that which is eternal within them. One headteacher I spoke to referred to the importance of his "hinterland" – the place and space where the soul is nourished, away from the necessary demands of the day job. Most headteachers I know have a hinterland they would happily spend hours telling you about; the problems come when they haven't been able to visit for a while. I spoke to another headteacher who was in his first year in post and said rather sadly that he hadn't played his fiddle for a long time. Make time and space for your hyacinths, your music, or your soul will starve.

PAUSE AND REFLECT

Let us ask ourselves two key questions:

⚑ What do we spend most of our time doing?

⚑ How does it match what should be our priorities?

---

[1] M. Fullan, *Leading in a Culture of Change* (San Francisco: Jossey-Bass, 2001), p. 7.

[2] YOUCAT, *Youth Catechism of the Catholic Church* (London: Catholic Truth Society, 2011), p. 176.

[3] Fullan, 2001, p. xiii.

[4] Heythrop Institute for Religion, Ethics and Public Life, *On the Way to Life* (London: Heythrop Institute for Religion, Ethics and Public Life, 2005), p. 23.

[5] B. Okri, "To an English Friend in Africa", from *An African Elegy* (London: Vintage, 1997).

[6] T. Brighouse, *How Successful Head Teachers Survive and Thrive* (Abingdon: RM Publications, 2007).

CHAPTER 8

Why Do You Do What You Do? – or, What's in Your Treasure Box?

I would like to turn now to an even deeper question, which is, "Why we do what we do in the first place?" Why do we put ourselves on the line in Catholic leadership and run the risks of public failure and ill health? I believe that if headteachers have a secure understanding of their motives for wanting to take the job on and are honest with themselves about their desires, then they will have a better chance of surviving the inevitable setbacks and challenges along the way. Many headteachers I spoke to tried to express their commitment to the role in terms of vocation, but it was clear to me that the thinking on vocation in Catholic leadership is very underdeveloped and has very fragile roots. There is no embedded orthodoxy of vocation or common language among headteachers. As we found in our examination of "New Vocations" in Chapter Two, the Church offers us very rich thinking on this subject, but it just hasn't found its way through to schools, either to the students or (most of) the leaders. Many headteachers could distinguish between a general vocation to discipleship, and headship as the current expression of that vocation, but there is clearly a pressing need for more work and support in this area.

The secular academic world can help us here, at least in the first stage of our exploration of motivation. The American psychologist David McClelland is credited with developing the influential theory of motivation, or theory of needs as it is sometimes known.[1] This theory has helped me understand why I do what I do and what I was looking to get out of it all along. I first came across this theory on the National College for School Leadership's programme for serving headteachers in 2004.

There are three social motives, the theory goes, which explain the widest range of human social behaviours: the "achievement motive", the "affiliation motive", and the "power motive". The Hay Group has also conducted extensive research on the relationship between underlying motivation and performance in organisations. Based on McClelland's work, I would characterise the three motives as follows:

The Achievement Motive

The need for achievement is an unconscious drive to do better towards a standard of excellence. People strongly motivated by achievement assess themselves to measure progress towards goals. They like frequent feedback, they prefer moderate risk rather

than low risk (no challenge), or high risk (danger of failure). They prefer working alone or with other high achievers and prefer individual recreational activities in which a person can get a score, like golf. They like occupations with lots of performance data. They also like being involved in long-term planning or advancement of career.

The Affiliation Motive

The need for affiliation is an unconscious drive to be part of warm, close relationships, like friendships. People strongly motivated by affiliation choose to spend time with close friends or significant others, prefer to work in groups, are sensitive to the reaction of others and prefer collaborative activities. They will conform easily to the norms of the group. They like to be liked.

The Power Motive

The need for power is an unconscious drive to have an impact on others. People with this motivation often assert themselves by taking leadership positions, gambling and committing aggressive acts. They prefer interpersonally competitive sports, such as football; they like to collect prestige possessions and prefer occupations in which they can have an impact on others. They like to influence, persuade or convince others to comply or conform rather than compromise or understand. They are concerned to impress the world at large and pay a great deal of attention to their reputation and status.

Which one best describes you? You may well recognise elements in yourself from all three motives.

The assumption is that we will have elements of all three but usually one dominant motivation. When I first came across these three types I was taken aback by how much I recognised in myself the achievement motive. There is a very helpful key to trying to determine the dominant motivation in a person. It is called a "behaviour event" question and it runs: "Tell me about a time recently when you felt effective in your job?" What the person says may well tell you a great deal about what motivates them. Governing bodies may wish to ask the question at the interview for their next headteacher. What kind of headteacher do you need for the next phase of the school's journey? Someone who can mend broken relationships, someone who can manage people assertively, or someone who is completely focused on achieving the gold medal?

We could also ask ourselves the "behaviour event" question to try and fathom the depths of our motivation. When we understand our motivation then we will better understand our thoughts and actions, since they are driven by our motivation. We act in ways which are driven by our motivations and avoid actions which are not. Do you recognise that from your own experience? Do we not all have a kind of internal prioritisation device which relegates our least attractive task to the bottom of the to-do list and before you know it ends up on tomorrow's list? Every motive is marked by a strong desire to reach a certain kind of goal – it's called a "goal state" – which is the feeling of satisfaction you get when it's achieved. This launches us on a cycle of satisfaction which looks like this:

MOTIVES underlie THOUGHTS which drive BEHAVIOURS geared towards

GOAL and GOAL-STATE ATTAINMENT.

Excitement feeds the desire to repeat this cycle, and behaviours become habitual.

The way we think, then act, prioritise our day, and deal with personal encounters is not neutral. It arises out of our default motivation, which is probably genetic. McClelland developed his research over years of working with many people in many professions, and he concluded that primary motives could change. According to McClelland, a person can change their motive by changing the way they think and act, but only if they want to change and only if there are what he calls "changes to the person's environmental supports". I think it is a compelling theory and stands up to our day-to-day experience. Whether or not we accept McClelland's work, we are still left with the challenge of recognising what drives us and *how* we look upon people and situations. As Christian leaders, we have been invited on a journey of slow transformation, so that we see situations and the people in front of us with "graced eyes". If we don't then we will continue to be looking either to dominate people, get them to like us, or use them to advance our own drive for achievement, or whatever mixture of those motivations drives us.

When I was invited to consider which motive best described me, I had to admit that I did get the most juice out of encounters and conversations which were directly related to achievement, innovative projects, improving performance and feedback about my own career. I know a number of colleagues, including former headteachers, who are an exact match for the power motive. I also know some colleagues who fit very well into the affiliation motive and spend a lot of their time trying to mend relationships or making sure they don't fracture in the first place. That is potentially dangerous territory for a Catholic school. In Chapter Five, I referred to the sensible approach of John Sullivan when he observed that the desire for good relations should never get in the way of running the school for the benefit of the students. We should never confuse *koinonia* (see Chapter Six for a definition of this) with a desire to make sure that all the adults in the community are happy. That is weak leadership. Nor should we confuse strong leadership with the desire to dominate others.

I think we can usefully bring a Christian perspective to this theory of social motives. Is there such a thing as a Christian motivation? We are bound to say that there has to be, otherwise Christian thinking and actions are only a surface feature of the person, rather than a deep-rooted motivation. If, as McClelland argues, motives can be changed by thinking and acting differently (which is no different to what the desert fathers say about training thoughts) then it would seem that we can develop and change to the point where our thoughts and actions arise out of a motivation to love God and love our neighbour. As we have done from the beginning, I would like to go back to the Gospel to try and outline the potential for a Christian understanding of the theory of social motives.

> ### PAUSE AND REFLECT
>
> ⚠ How would describe your main motivation for doing what you do?
>
> ⚠ When do you feel most effective?

Your Treasure Box

In Matthew's Gospel Jesus says, "Where your treasure is, there your heart will be also" (6:21). It is an interesting formulation and is often carelessly rendered as where your heart is there will your treasure be, but that's not what Jesus said. He said you need to start with the treasure. There is a wonderful meditation on this by Denis McBride in his CD set, *Jesus and the Gospels* (which I would also add to your shopping basket). McBride starts with the observation that if you want to know the content of someone's heart, you don't look in their heart, you look in their treasure box. What is it they value most? In terms of the discussion above, we could ask, "What is their main motivation?" For some people it

certainly is a sense of achievement. That is their chief treasure and that is what educates their heart.

But the Christian reading of this psychology goes on to ask, "Is it good for the heart to be schooled by an overwhelming drive towards achievement?" If that is what determines one's behaviour and interactions with other people, it seems to be a long way from the Gospel. On the surface, the motivation of affiliation looks closer to the Gospel, but if you look at the behaviour of Jesus he was not primarily driven by the need to make everybody feel happy. He was not concerned about what people thought of him. There were times when what he said drove people away, but he had the courage to say what was in his heart. Nor was he motivated by power. This is evident in the story of the temptation in the wilderness (see Luke 4:1-13), where Jesus rejected any kind of dominating power, but grew beyond these motivations to something much more enduring.

The point that McBride makes very powerfully is that if you don't have something in your treasure box which is everlasting then you could be in trouble. If your chief treasure is to achieve, then what happens when you stop achieving? That day will come, that much is certain, and your heart will break. If your chief treasure is to make everybody like you, what happens when you're among a group of wholly indifferent people? Your heart will wither. If your chief treasure is power, what happens when someone more powerful comes along? If we turn to the Gospel of Matthew, we find that Jesus advises us not to clutter our treasure boxes with earthly things, "where moth and rust consume and where thieves break in and steal" (6:19). Rather he says we should store up treasure in heaven. What about Jesus himself? Having thrown out the temptations of power and status, what was in his treasure box that gave him such natural authority and such a passion for his mission?

McBride turns to the mysterious story of the transfiguration for the answer. He acknowledges that this is one of the most problematic pieces of scripture for scholars. No one is quite sure if it is historical, legendary, or a resurrection story which appears in the wrong place. It begins with Jesus going up the mountain with his inner circle. In Matthew's account, which provides more detail than Mark's, it says that Jesus was transfigured before them and "his face shone like the sun" (17:2). But it is in Luke's account that we have the closest link with prayer, which is the key to his treasure. He tells us that Jesus went up the mountain to pray and, "while he was praying, the appearance of his face changed" (Luke 9:29).

McBride reads this as an event in which Jesus encounters Abba, his Father, and is convinced that he is loved. When the clouds part the voice says, "This is my Son, my Chosen" (9:35). It is compelling to consider this episode as the community's memory of Jesus having a mystical experience in which he is made radiant by the love of his Father. Moments like this give him his authority and drive him on to complete his mission in the face of risk and hostility. His treasure is the enduring and faithful love of his Father and this is what we are invited to have in our treasure box. Everything else is contingent, conditional, flawed. The love of God is eternal and will not rust or be stolen. Love is what transfigures and transforms; the absence of love is what

disfigures. For those who wish to extend their Bible study, notice that, in all the synoptic Gospels following the transfiguration scene, you will see a "disfigured son" being healed and transformed by the "transfigured Son", Jesus.

For Catholic leaders this is what must sustain us. We cannot expect to be mission leaders without this foundation. And how can we find that motivation, or treasure? Like Jesus, we have to pray and grow as disciples. We will bring our default motivation to our leadership role but we must grow beyond that on a journey of discipleship by committing to a personal relationship with God. If that is our chief treasure then we will be able to cope better with the trials, the dark days of crisis. We will also articulate the mission of the school out of a personal faith. It will not be the end of everything if we have a bad set of results, or somebody doesn't like us, or one day they don't do what we tell them to because we don't seem as powerful any more. One former headteacher, still in a leadership role in Catholic education, put it this way:

I believe passionately in the need for space and time and quiet and prayer and all of those things, because otherwise you get blown this way and that; so how are you creating that space by which God can work through you? It's what St Augustine said, "God is within and we are outside of ourselves," – it's a kind of frightening concept really and I think it's that idea of the inner journey being absolutely a prerequisite of leadership within our tradition

Former Headteacher

Why Pray, How to Pray

If prayer is the process by which we slowly surrender to the love of God, or get inside of ourselves as St Augustine said, and we see our ego diminish so that, as St Paul says in his Letter to the Galatians, "it is no longer I who live, but it is Christ who lives in me" (Galatians 2:20), then prayer becomes the necessary activity of the Catholic headteacher. None of this should come as much of a surprise. Catholic leaders after all inhabit reserved posts, and on the tin it says we should be practising Catholics, which should involve something more than weekly Mass attendance.

I enjoy leading the staff and students in prayer and I have received far more than I have given in terms of prayer resources and experiences, but when it comes to devoting regular time to prayer I am barely in the novice category. In my visits to schools I was humbled and inspired by one headteacher whose inner city school was in a "category" and faced the perfect storm of a historically bad reputation, falling roll, falling budget and a new free school just down the road. Her energy, enthusiasm and, yes, hope, were infectious. Without prompting, she told me about her prayer life. She rose at 5.30 a.m. (as Jesus often did) and spent half an hour in prayer before the house stirred. (She did say that it was only really possible now that her children were a bit older, but then mine are a bit older as well and I don't use the gained time in the morning to rise and pray.) She used the online prayer resource developed by the Jesuits in Ireland (**www.sacredspace.ie**) which has proved so popular. For her, prayer was a daily necessity, a "lifeline", as she called it.

The huge highlighted spreadsheet on the wall of her office told of the considerable efforts she went to in order to ensure that Year Eleven students left with the best possible grades. A return visit from Ofsted was just around the corner, the school faced a constant battle to convince the local (Catholic) community that this was a very good school, and there was little prospect of capital funding to help set up a sixth form unless the school could become an academy, which it couldn't do in its current category; but all of this was somehow more manageable because she prayed. As she showed me round the school there was a palpable sense of energy and determination from everybody to make the school succeed, but I was most struck by the attitude of the headteacher. I did not get the impression that she was driven by achievement, the need to be loved, or power, but that her love for her students and her mission were funded by her own deep sense of being loved by God.

Most headteachers were not as comfortable talking about their spiritual lives. It is part of the British psyche to be reserved in such matters. My sense is that many headteachers rely on their own resources, often from a "cradle" Catholic upbringing, when it comes to prayer. Most Catholics were brought up with a rich repertoire of prayers, but were left with a largely underdeveloped understanding of the techniques, theology or purpose of prayer. I observed in a previous chapter that one of the most powerful characteristics of our schools is that we pray. Our children pray and in my experience of speaking to many of them they enjoy the experience. But do *we* pray? Do we pray enough? And what do we understand by prayer? Again it was not an area that many headteachers felt inclined to open up about,

but my own perception is that we have mostly an unsupported and underdeveloped understanding of prayer. One of the biggest traps we can fall into as Catholics is prayer by rote, rattling through the words we know so well, as if that had anything to do with inner transformation.

Enzo Bianchi, a lay Italian Catholic who founded a monastic community in Bose, northern Italy, has produced a beautiful little book called *Why Pray, How to Pray*. It is written after many years of prayer and reflection. Steeped in scripture, drawing on the wisdom of the desert fathers and the wider tradition of the Church, it is an ideal primer for those who wish to come to a more mature understanding of what prayer is all about. Bianchi sums it up as follows:

The aim of prayer, in fact, is to attain that point where we do the will of God, not that God should do our will. Our prayers do not change the plan of God's love for us, but it is the gifts which God grants in prayer which transform us and which bring us into harmony with his will.[2]

Richard Rohr arrives at much the same conclusion. In *Yes, and…*, he summarises his understanding of prayer as follows:

The word prayer has often been trivialized by making it into a way of getting what we want. But I use the word prayer as the umbrella word for any interior journeys or practices that allow you to experience faith, hope and love within yourself. It is not a technique for getting things, a pious exercise that somehow makes God happy, or a requirement for entry into heaven. It is much more like practising heaven now.[3]

Pope Francis, in "The Joy of the Gospel", seems to have a similar approach, almost as if he is gently trying to coax us out of a childish belief in prayer as the divine slot machine model which many of us were brought up with:

We can say that God's heart is touched by our intercession, yet in reality he is always there first. What our intercession achieves is that his power, his love and his faithfulness are shown ever more clearly in the midst of the people.[4]

If I am reading this correctly it is a similar position to Bianchi's and Rohr's, in that the purpose of prayer is not to change the mind of God about the course of human history, but to live a little more in the life of the Spirit and to see the world a little clearer with graced eyes. Prayer is more about the effect on us rather than the effect on God: "When evangelizers rise from prayer, their hearts are more open; freed of self-absorption, they are desirous of doing good and sharing their lives with others."[5] Pope Francis cites St Paul as an example of a Christian whose prayers were full of people and concludes that true contemplation always has a place for others. He makes a particular point that will appeal to all Catholic headteachers when he invites us to pray for those whom we find most difficult. After your next staff meeting think of these words: "To pray for a person with whom I am irritated is a beautiful step forward in love."[6]

As for the techniques of prayer, *how* to pray, that is beyond the scope of this book but I would highly recommend Richard Rohr, especially *The Naked Now*, and Enzo Bianchi's book as two very fruitful starting points. The religious orders have their own traditions. We have briefly mentioned the Jesuit tradition based on the spirituality of St Ignatius of Loyola. I would also encourage all colleagues to discover *Lectio Divina* (the prayerful reflection on scripture) if they have not done so already. I was introduced to it very powerfully in the course of my research. I'd heard of *Lectio* but never paid it much attention. During my visit to an independent boarding school I was invited at the end of my interviews to join the headmaster and some students for *Lectio Divina*. The format is relatively simple: invocation to the Holy Spirit, recognition of our sinfulness, reading of a passage of scripture, followed by the sharing of "echoes", or what the passage meant for us, then bidding prayers. There are variations of this format but this seemed to work very well. I was so moved by the experience I suggested to our cluster group of Catholic heads that we introduced it before our next meeting. Eight of my colleagues agreed to meet half an hour before our meeting was due to start for *Lectio*. It has now become an established part of our routine.

The Art of Accompaniment

We pay such a lot of attention, and rightly so, to the accompaniment of our young people on their journey. We should also be paying a great deal more attention, in my view, to the accompaniment of our leaders. Many headteachers did say that they would welcome more opportunities for spiritual nourishment. We are asking our leaders to be faith leaders but do we give them the support and formation they need to fulfil that role? When I was fourteen years old at junior seminary in the north of Scotland the Church thought so much of me that I was provided with a spiritual director. I remember him well. He was a saintly Irish priest, with a great devotion to Our Lady and an endless patience with the pathologies of working-class boys two hundred miles from home. I am now a fifty-one-year-old Catholic headteacher with nothing like the same spiritual support. We have our own informal networks and my diocese does what it can to support us, but in terms of national interest in a systematic spiritual accompaniment for such a critical post, I was not aware of much going on.

It was this deficit which prompted a group of us to organise the first national retreat for Catholic headteachers in 2011. A retreat is not a conference. There is a very important difference. Headteachers are well used to conferences: keynote speakers, networking over coffee, nice hotel rooms, too much time in the bar after dinner. A retreat will have some of those features but the emphasis has to be on spiritual stimulation, nourishment and prayer. Our first retreat was led by Fr Denis McBride who provided us with wonderful insights into the Gospels as studies in human leadership. The second retreat was led by Fr Christopher Jamison who opened up for us the tradition of the desert fathers and the importance of not being dominated by bad thoughts – so important in the mental frenzy that is modern headship. The third retreat was led by Fr Timothy Radcliffe who shared his memorable insights on the theme of life to the full. The retreat involves reconciliation services, adoration of the blessed sacrament and space and time for private prayer. Those who have attended very much appreciated what was for many the first real opportunity in the academic year to have any kind of retreat or reflection.

In the Gospels, the evangelists emphasise the importance of personal prayer in the life of Jesus. His public ministry is marked by many references to retreats, especially early in the morning when he goes off by himself. He is the role model *par excellence* for all those who struggle with the theft of time. This is the real hinterland we should visit frequently. Our soul will be nourished by time spent on what makes us more human – be that reading, hill walking, or rowing on a quiet river as the sun comes up (as one of my headteacher friends does in the summer) – our soul will be nourished by attentive time spent with our nearest and dearest; but above all our soul needs to be nourished by time spent in prayer and communion with the divine, as Jesus exemplifies in the Gospels. I was very struck by a statement in Enzo Bianchi's book which at first I thought was too strong. "It has to be said clearly: *anyone who claims not to have time for prayer in reality is confessing to idolatry*".[7] I think he's right. If we're saying that we have no time for prayer then we are in fact saying that all of the other things we're doing today are more important than prayer. It is a remarkable comment from another of the prophets of the age and prophets, as we've always known, are the ones who makes us feel uncomfortable.

A natural progression from the national retreat was the aspiration to provide spiritual accompaniment for Catholic headteachers. At the 2014 retreat, a pilot programme called Emmaus was launched in partnership between EducareM and the Jesuit Institute to offer spiritual direction to around twenty headteachers in the north-west of England and in London. I hope that as you read this the programme is alive and well and spreading to other parts of the country. I believe that the spiritual formation and accompaniment of our headteachers should be our first priority. Writing in 2002, Gerald Grace identified the "spiritual capital" of our future Catholic leaders as the biggest challenge to the mission integrity of our schools. Grace's extensive research among secondary headteachers revealed a cohort of leaders with well-stocked reserves of spiritual capital, derived largely from their upbringing:

The sources of their own spiritual capital have included the significant effects of their own secondary schooling and college experiences (the influence of religious orders being prominent), a family background of prayer and regular attendance at Mass, their own current prayer life and religious practice, and professional opportunities for development and reflection upon the spiritual context of Catholic schooling.[8]

My own research, among a smaller sample and with much less academic rigour, found this still to be the case, although a number of colleagues pointed out that "cradle" Catholicism (which is what Grace describes above) was not in itself enough and they had to embark on personal faith journeys. A traditional Catholic upbringing certainly gave them the framework and resources for such a journey and I think it's the absence of that framework in the up-and-coming generation which concerns Grace the most. His thesis is that this spiritual capital has been the dynamic driving force of the mission of our schools. The critical question facing the Church today then is how do we form and nourish future generations of Catholic school leaders and teachers who are less likely to have benefited from the sources of spiritual capital available to previous generations?

We are caught up here in a larger sweep of secularisation and the consequent "crisis of transmission" referred to in an earlier chapter. The Catholic culture which provided this capital and formed so many of the current and previous generations of Catholic leaders – the vibrant parishes, church-going inter-generational families, clubs,

societies and opportunities for faith formation – is rapidly disappearing. So what are we to do? It is true that as a Church we must devote what resources we can to ensure that Catholic leaders continue to benefit from the spiritual capital of the past, but there is a danger of that becoming entirely a cerebral exercise. What I would argue for is a focus not just on spiritual capital, but on *spiritual life*.

If our current and future leaders are to survive and thrive and preserve the mission integrity of our schools against the political assaults which will surely come, and worse still the enervating apathy towards religion which is now endemic, then they need something more in their treasure box than knowledge of the tradition. They need a "missionary heart" as Francis calls it; they need to be disciples of Jesus Christ who are on a personal journey of transformation which is funded by personal and communal prayer. To sustain our leaders we will still need our programmes of leadership but above all we will need a *school of formation*. If the Church helped to develop an understanding of Catholic leadership as a *ministry*, then I'm sure the need for formation would be obvious.

I remember speaking to one of our colleagues who helped to organise the three-month retreat programme at Hawkstone Hall run by the Redemptorists. She said they had many Australian Catholic headteachers with them who were on three-month sabbaticals. I am so pleased that our Australian colleagues can benefit from such enrichment but it must be noted with some concern that our own headteachers are not there. A school of formation could take many formats: a three-month residential programme for headteachers on sabbatical promoted by all the dioceses of England and Wales would be ideal, but perhaps too big a step to begin with. Colleagues in the past have developed formats involving a short residential at the beginning and end of the year with online resources, accompaniment, reading and reflection in between. Such a "school" could teach our leaders how to pray, how to read the scriptures, how to understand and interpret the tradition for the "cool" generation. With due respect to our fine academics, it would be better located outside the parameters of academic accreditation, since formation of this kind cannot be weighed and measured. I appreciate that some dioceses have attempted to run such innovative programmes but I'm not aware of any sustained success or any impetus towards such an approach at the national level.

If a school of formation is too much to ask, then at the very least we need more opportunities to meet and support each other with the sharing of insights and resources. Most professional associations would have a webforum for online discussion, a bank of online resources, and regular sharing of good practice. Some dioceses are able to provide some of this, but now may be the favourable time to strengthen our national network. As an educational community we should give this matter our most urgent attention if we wish to have a Catholic educational system to pass on to our children. The structural politics of how such opportunities might be created and run may well be enough to bury the idea, as often happens, but the emergence of a national retreat and the beginnings of a national programme of spiritual accompaniment should give us hope.

Should I Stay or Should I go?

Priests retire at seventy (although many work on), bishops at seventy-five and cardinals don't get a vote in the Sistine Chapel after the age of eighty. Catholic headteachers, though, like other headteachers in the state sector in England and Wales currently have a normal retirement age of sixty, but are able to take early retirement with a reduced pension from the age of fifty-five (although that seems about to change if the government gets its way). Around half of the headteachers I spoke to intended to retire before the age of sixty, with two about to retire at the age of fifty-five. Both of them confirmed that the constant pressure of accountability, the pace of change, and the damage they had seen done to friends and colleagues in the role were key factors in their decision. I have been a Catholic headteacher in maintained secondary schools for twelve years and I somehow don't see myself continuing until I'm sixty. Why not? Because it takes chunks out of you. It's a wonderful job, but it does tear at your natural fabric. So how long can anyone reasonably be expected to last in headship, what does the research tell us about effectiveness, and what are the implications for our schools and the Church?

In *How Successful Head Teachers Survive and Thrive*[9], Tim Brighouse outlines and defines four stages of headship – *initiation*, *development*, *stall* and *decline*. They can be paraphrased as follows:

Initiation

This stage is the first encounter between the new head and the stakeholders. In this phase the newly appointed headteacher is often listening, getting to know the community and then leading a review of the mission and priorities. The great benefit a new headteacher can bring to a school is *fresh eyes* – how long has *this* been going on? With the best will in the world you do stop seeing things after a while. This is why there is a different order of challenge for internal appointments. This phase is all about first impressions, first messages. It is also the phase where many first-time headteachers find their public voice. Deputy headteachers will speak often enough in public but not always as the "official" voice of the school. That tends to be a role reserved for the headteacher. That first open evening for a new headteacher is critical, as some of my colleagues were well aware:

You can't wear your stress on your sleeve so you've got to carry assurance and confidence and you've got to be decisive and you've got to be a presence. You can't run a decent open evening with some diffident person mumbling away behind a paper, behind a podium, behind a microphone.

Sixth Form College Principal

In this phase it is critical to establish yourself in the eyes of the community as a credible leader; or, in the terms we have been using, an authentic Catholic leader with a personal faith which inspires your vision for the school. In this phase of headship the constellation of energy-enthusiasm-hope has to be at its brightest. Different schools will have different needs; for some it will require a rocket, for others it may be more evolution than revolution but they will all need *drive* from the new leaders. In the next chapter we will look at the six leadership styles described by Daniel Goleman. Another big decision is which leadership style best suits this school at this time and how can I provide that in a Christian way? In my interviews I asked the headteachers, whose experience in office ranged from one year to twenty years, to provide some advice for the newly appointed (see "Top Tips for Tyros" on page 98).

Development

In this phase the head is known and all the effort is concentrated on putting into place the agreed aims and priorities for making the school even more effective, or making the mission a deeper reality. There are many different views about how long it takes to make a difference, turn around a school, or change the culture. It will depend a lot on circumstances. My first headship was two and a half years and I think a lot of good work was done which was built upon by my successors. I am still in my second substantive headship ten years on and I would say it took around four years to change the culture in the ways that were necessary. Brighouse refers to research carried out by Peter Mortimore, which suggests that heads are at their best between the third and seventh years. Colleagues reading this in their eighth year and beyond, however, should not despair. Brighouse goes on to say that the development stage can be repeated.

Stall

The third phase is the risk of *stall*. The development stage is typically complete between five and seven years and then there is the danger that you think the school can run on autopilot and you can become more interested in developments and opportunities outside of school. That rings very true in my experience. I have felt, and given in, to the temptation to be drawn out of school by projects which I could easily convince myself would benefit the school. In this phase bad habits can creep in, especially if there is no pressure from Ofsted regarding your category. This is when you can coast and become complacent.

Brighouse does not suggest you need to go at this point. He rightly says that you can change gear and start another development stage. It's at this stage that you could ask your governors for a sabbatical to attend the *school of formation* so you can come back refreshed for another stage of development. The problem we have in this county is that there is no precedent or structure for sabbaticals in most dioceses, so most governing bodies will struggle with such a request. But we are missing an opportunity to help our headteachers thrive. I would encourage all governing bodies to consider giving headteachers who have been in post for seven or more years at least a three-month sabbatical, as they do in Australia.

The more of these development stages you do the more difficult it becomes to sustain that energy-enthusiasm-hope that we started with. All schools should aim to be outstanding and either to lead a school to that status, or maintain and develop it, requires a leader who is *on it*, every day, with relentless focus. I am aware of the tension between that comment and all my comments above about sacred time. One will not exclude the other; in fact with the rising level of pressure and challenge, the

need for sacred time becomes critical. I have heard Brighouse remark in another context that the era of the twenty-year headship is over. There will still be exceptional individuals who can sustain excellence for such a long period but I think Brighouse is right. He says that in twenty-year headships you seldom find that the second ten years were as effective as the first ten.

My own view is that the ideal shift in headship is around ten years. That gives you time to develop and deepen the Catholic culture of the school over successive years, to really get to know the community, to lead any major structural developments which might have been necessary. But you also have to give the community a chance to renew itself under new leadership, with fresh eyes, and renew *yourself* with another headship, or another role in the Church. There may come a point when your best thinking no longer holds the attention of your community, when your message becomes a bit tired, when you stop seeing what needs to be done. It requires a great deal of courage and self-awareness to know when the time has come to move on.

Decline

When you have decided to go, go quickly. Servant leaders should not need any farewell tour or long periods of appreciation. It was never about you, but about the children and young people who get one shot at their formation and education. The period of decline is when the head has either publically stated he or she is going, or else it is painfully obvious that in their heart they have gone, but they haven't quite found something else to go to yet. Heads should remember that they are "stewards of God's mysteries", and the growth, life chances, and opportunities for our young people to encounter the living Gospel in our schools rely to a large extent on the quality of leadership. If you are getting in the way of that then you need to move. Go quietly, go with dignity, and stay gone. The last thing your successor needs is you hanging around like a ghost at the banquet. They'll manage somehow without you.

And then what will you do? In the course of this research it has struck me that there will be a cohort of very capable Catholic leaders in their mid to late fifties and sixties who will have retired and who will not always find a role for themselves in the Church, who will be looking for the next expression of their vocation. I know of one forward-thinking diocese which has a cadre of retired headteachers working for them to offer support and guidance. To me it is a waste of our most valuable resource if we just let our headteachers retire and lose touch with them. I suspect that if there was more encouragement from the Church to think of headship as a ministry of service, then it would be more natural for them to continue in that service beyond headship.

One of my favourite mantras comes from the Jewish tradition and it runs something like, *If you want to make God laugh, tell him your plans.* As headteachers we spend a lot of time drawing up plans and we often take that mindset into our own lives, planning the next career move. As Christians we must remember that we are not in charge. "New Vocations" reminds us that when we are trying to discern the lineaments of our vocation, or what we should do next, "the fundamental requirement is the person's level of

docibilitas",[10] which is the freedom to let ourselves be guided.

Pope Francis also reminds us that we should not worry too much about the limitations of our own resources, which will always in some sense be found wanting, nor should we ever give in to despondency: "While painfully aware of our own frailties, we have to march on without giving in, keeping in mind what the Lord said to Saint Paul: 'My grace is sufficient for you, for my power is made perfect in weakness' (2 Corinthians 12:9)."[11]

Top Tips for Tyros

I asked a number of the headteachers if they had any advice for colleagues who were just embarking on the journey of headship. Here are some of their words of wisdom:

My advice would be, work out what you think is really going to benefit the children; how dare you take their time, this precious thing, they can't get it back, it's their childhood you've got in their hands, so what are you going to do with that? Never mind about the government, never mind about Ofsted, why is that little boy going past my door now better off because he's here today? If you can't answer that, work bloody hard until you can and stick to it, and that's leadership.

Primary Headteacher

I'd say first and foremost only go for it if you really, really want it. I would say you have to have a real love and passion, not just for teaching, but for your faith. You have to acknowledge the fact that you're leading a faith community, not just leading a school, and I would say your guiding light, apart from the good Lord, will be your mission statement and aims, which you have to subscribe to a hundred per cent because you'll be expecting everybody else to.

Primary Headteacher

My advice to new heads is based entirely on Bathsheba taking over the farm in Far from the Madding Crowd. She speaks to everyone on the farm and asks them, "What do you do?" and that's what I did and the answers are more complicated that you can imagine, just as they are in the novel. You would think that it's the head who tells everyone what to do but in fact the first job I had to do was to find out from everyone what they did.

Secondary Headteacher

One needs time to listen to people, to look, like a good doctor. The essence of being a good doctor is to observe, to look at what the patient needs and then make up your mind what's going to happen and you can't rush into that diagnosis and it's a diagnosis on yourself as well – Who am I as a headteacher because I've never been this before? How do I want to lead? What do I want to talk about? That needs time and be prepared for people to say, "She hasn't done much yet. She's not very active, not like the last one!"

Secondary Headteacher

Your Top 10 Resolutions to Ensure You Survive and Thrive in Headship

Most headteachers make lists, sometimes they make a list of the lists they need to make. I use lists sometimes as displacement activity when I should be doing what's on the list. One list which might benefit you is ten things you could do, or do better, which would improve your chances of surviving and thriving in headship, in whatever phase you face next. Here's one I prepared earlier:

1. Go on retreat.
2. Take Sundays off.
3. Visit your hinterland.
4. Don't open emails after 7 p.m.
5. Develop the habit of spiritual reading.
6. Make time for daily prayer – sacred time.
7. Work from home some days – make time for "slow thinking".
8. Walk your school every day you're in: people not paper.
9. Engage in some action research by visiting other schools.
10. After seven years in post ask your governors for a proper sabbatical of at least three months.

[1] David C. McClelland, *Human Motivation* (Cambridge: Cambridge University Press, 1988).
[2] E. Bianchi, *Why Pray, How to Pray* (London: St Paul's, 2014), p. 49.
[3] R. Rohr, *Yes, and…* (Cincinnati: Franciscan Media, 2013), p. 7.
[4] *Evangelii Gaudium*, 283.
[5] Ibid., 282.
[6] Ibid., 101.
[7] Bianchi, 2014, p. 85.
[8] G. Grace, *Catholic Schools: Mission, Markets and Morality* (Abingdon: Routledge Falmer, 2002), p. 237.
[9] T. Brighouse, *How Successful Head Teachers Survive and Thrive* (Abingdon: RM Publications, 2007).
[10] *In Verbo Tuo*.
[11] *Evangelii Gaudium*, 85.

CHAPTER 9

What Lies in Wait – Catholic Leadership in a Culture of Change

If you want some sense of what has happened to the human race in the last twenty years, and what might be facing us in the next twenty, have a look at the original *Shift Happens* video on YouTube (**www.youtube.com**). It was made by the California State University in 2006 to stimulate a discussion with the staff of one school about the components of a twenty-first-century education. It is currently running at around five million views, with multiple spin-offs and versions. It captures the *zeitgeist* with striking statistics and observations:

- The number one English-speaking country in the world will soon be China.

- The US Department of Labor estimates that today's teenagers will have between 10 and 14 jobs by their 38th birthday.

- Today's 21-year-olds have watched 20,000 hours of television, played 10,000 hours of video games and sent or received 250,000 texts or emails.

- More than 50% of US 21-year-olds have created content on the internet.

- 70% of four-year-olds in the US have used a computer.

- The internet first became widely available to the public in 1995.

- In the US in 2013 one in eight couples who married met online.

- 2.7 billon searches were carried out on Google in July 2014 – what happened to those searches B.G. (before Google)?

- Technical information is doubling every two years.

- 2 billion children live in developing countries.

- One in three never complete fifth grade (Year Six in England and Wales).

- In 2005 the One Laptop per Child Project (OLPC) set out to provide laptops for these children.

- By the 2040s we will have developed a supercomputer with the same computational capacity as the human race.

- We are currently preparing students for jobs using technologies that don't yet exist in order to solve problems we don't know are problems yet.

Some of the facts and figures relate to the United States, some are global, but the assumption is that in the United Kingdom we are living through the same pattern of rapid change and our figures will not be dissimilar. It's the kind of presentation you might get at a national conference which leaves you simultaneously stirred and shaken as a school leader. You feel the pace and pressure of change, and you wonder what you can do about any of it in your little corner of the country.

There is no escaping the fact that we are living in times of exponential change. We have experienced a generational shift which is bigger than rock and roll. When I graduated in the mid-1980s none of us had seen or used a computer, imagined the internet, or possessed a mobile phone; we had to wait our turn to use the one telephone in the house, or gather up 10p coins to make a call in a vandalised telephone box in the street. Now we have children coming into reception class who pick up a book and swipe the page, because they are more used to a tablet device than a book made of paper. Most children no longer wear a watch, because it is, after all, a single-function device: they have mobile phones to tell them the time, and take pictures, and play music, as well as provide them with a messaging service, diary, calculator, games, alarm clock, daily news, compass, torch (oh yes, and an entire library…).

We looked in Chapter Seven at the dark side of the new technology as a time thief, but we shouldn't settle for a Luddite position. We do have to hold on to what is essential and indeed eternal, but we also have to lead the change in our schools and respond to what our young people will need. The questions I would like to consider in this chapter are: To what extent are we

in Catholic education able to meet the challenges of educating children to be successful in twenty-first-century society? Are our schools fit for purpose? Are our leaders able to lead in such a culture of change, or is our vision of education hopelessly moribund in a language that no one pays attention to any more?

The Church has not always engaged enthusiastically with the modern world, often seeing itself as a haven, an ark of truth on the seething waters of worldly corruption. We have had good reason in recent times to be somewhat more humble. We have moved on but in the minds of many the Church is still seen as a superstitious medieval organisation, which does not regard science or technology as particularly important in comparison to the care of souls. Vatican II did a great deal to open the Church to dialogue with the modern world but old habits die hard. The first danger facing us as educational leaders is that we subscribe to an atavistic view of the modern age as hopelessly decadent and don't see ourselves as *in* it and *of* it, with much to offer to those who are seeking to navigate the best course in unchartered waters. Previous popes have sometimes reinforced a negative view of contemporary society, employing a rhetoric of the struggle for the world's soul, or of the tyranny of moral relativism. Pope Francis invites us to take a view which is perhaps more balanced:

Every period of history is marked by the presence of human weakness, self-absorption, complacency and selfishness, to say nothing of the concupiscence which preys upon us all… Let us not say, then, that things are harder today; they are simply different.[1]

Today's society is not perfect, we are very well aware of some of the shocking behaviour around us, but in fact it is really no better or worse than previous generations. There was really no golden age of moral consensus. Some generations in the past were certainly subject to greater conventional controls, but to say it was better or for that matter more *Christian*, no longer sounds very convincing. The headteachers I have spoken to seem to be very much in tune with Francis. There was no sense of moral outrage at the state of modern society or its young people. There was a profound awareness of the challenges we face, and for some communities in this country they are acute, but nevertheless they showed a remarkable optimism in the face of the challenges, or, to go back to our supernatural virtues, a steadfast *hope*.

So what kind of skills and qualities do our children and young people need to leave school with in order to survive and thrive in this brave new world of exponential technological change? Ken Robinson, in the new edition of his best-selling book, *Out of Our Minds*, provides a very compelling summary of what the business world is telling us to cultivate in our young people. You would have thought that with modern economies so dependent on the new technologies, business leaders would be asking for greater technical and functional IT skills from the young workforce, perhaps more computing in schools? Apparently not. Robinson, who has many years of experience working with a wide range of businesses and educational systems across the world, reports that:

when I talk with business leaders, they complain that education isn't producing the thoughtful, creative, self-confident people they urgently need: people who are literate, numerate, who can analyse information and ideas; who can generate new ideas of their own and help to implement them; who can communicate clearly and work well with other people.[2]

It would seem that what we call "soft" skills (as well as the core competencies) are most in demand, according to Robinson.

Over the years, Robinson has been scathingly critical of an education system which has generally not produced enough young people with these qualities. For busy headteachers, there is an excellent animated summary of his thesis on the RSA (Royal Society for the encouragement of Arts, Manufactures and Commerce) website (**www.thersa.org**) called Changing Paradigms. (The RSA Animate series is well worth a visit: like the TED lectures it presents the best of modern thinking on a range of issues in a highly entertaining way.) Robinson's point in a nutshell is that our education system remains largely unchanged from the industrial model which emerged in the nineteenth century to serve the needs of that society: a fixed view of intelligence, a curriculum imposed from the centre which divided students sharply into academic or vocational categories, taught by teachers whose main role was to deliver knowledge, organised in same-age groups, with stressful standardised tests at the end. No wonder we have seen increasing disaffection among our students, with undiscovered talents and a sense of pass or fail at the end. Robinson argues that the main casualty of this system is a young person's self-esteem and well-being because their creativity and identity have not been allowed to flourish. The other casualty is the economy, because we are left with such a shortage of young people who have the qualities outlined above.

This of course is highly political territory. In this country we have an educational system which can be influenced to an extraordinary degree by one person, the Secretary of State for Education. His or her own education and vision can determine what is taught in our schools. The inspection regime then monitors the extent to which we are implementing that vision. Headteachers do not always feel they have much room for manoeuvre, but Robinson's vision will resonate with Catholic headteachers and encourage us on a path which the Church has in fact been advocating for some years. He says that creative teaching or teaching *for* creativity is the key to nurturing the best skills in our students. His description of this kind of teaching will be recognised by many of our school leaders:

Teaching for creativity involves asking open-ended questions where there may be multiple solutions, working in groups on collaborative projects, using imagination to explore possibilities; making connections between different ways of seeing; and exploring the ambiguous tensions that may lie between them.[3]

There are three related tasks in teaching for creativity: *encouraging*, *identifying* and *developing*. Schools must pay more attention, Robinson argues, to encouraging their students to discover their own creativity and to overcome the barriers of doubt and insecurity which may have been in place since birth; identifying their creative strength; and developing not just the special gifts of the students but the wider skills of team work, enquiry, expression and critical thinking. As we noted earlier, there is a strong convergence here with "New Vocations", which also encourages us to find the "original gift" in our students and to develop five pedagogical attitudes to help them on their journey towards the personal fulfilment of their calling: to sow the seed (*encouraging*); to accompany (*encouraging*); to educate (*identifying*); to form (*identifying*); to discern (*developing*). I am not suggesting that Ken Robinson is a secret fan of "New Vocations" (he may well be, although I doubt it) but he is on a very similar path.

Robinson sums up his educational vision as "personalisation". This approach has received a good deal of attention in this country since the then Secretary of State for Education David Miliband promoted the idea in a speech in 2004.[4] It has now become something of the norm in the commercial sector (as we saw in the Stephen Covey example in Chapter Three), customising the service to the needs of the customer ("My M&S", and the like). Personalisation in education is an approach which should sit very comfortably with Catholic schools. In the Judeo-Christian tradition there is a strong understanding of being called by God "by name" (Isaiah 43:1). A mysterious passage from the Book of Revelation describes a white stone, "and on the white stone is written a new name that no one knows except the one who receives it" (Revelation 2:17). We are unique, loved and called. This tradition of personalisation, however, has not always been the dominant philosophy in modern western theories of education, even though the foundations were Christian.

There has been a faultline running through education for more than a century between what Robinson calls the "Enlightenment" tradition and the "Romantic" tradition. The former, sometimes known as the "rationalist" world view, favours certain qualities of mind, above all, logic and deduction. Education should therefore focus on processes that promote a rational state of mind, which is developed through absorbing bodies of knowledge. The main role of teachers is to transmit that knowledge. The only growing the student does is acquiring knowledge and a rationalist approach to the world with a view to gaining civic virtue. The Romantic view on the other hand, or "natural individualism", assumes that every child is by nature a unique individual with innate talents and sensibilities. Education should draw out these qualities rather than suppress them and should not be knowledge-based but child-centred. Those with their finger on the pulse will recognise the tussle which continues in government today about the better approach. Those who favour the so-called rigours of the rationalist approach often look to the booming economies of Asia as examples of success. Before returning to what the Church can offer in this debate, I would like to share some of my own recent experiences of the Chinese educational system, to see if this is the model we need to emulate to manage the changes that lie in wait.

New World Order

The attention of western educationalists turned east in 2001 when the first set of test results from the Programme for International Student Assessment (PISA) showed that the star performers were not the "old" countries of Europe but the emerging economies of Asia. In the 2012 tests, published in 2013, the top five regions with the highest mean scores in maths were, in order: Shanghai, Singapore, Hong Kong, Taiwan and South Korea (see **www.oecd.org/pisa/keyfindings** for a very interesting overview of the results). The United Kingdom scored around average for maths, and just above average for reading and science. For an ambitious politician, that's not good enough. The tests are not without controversy and some argue that the students in the most successful regions are prepared with great rigour for the tests (sounds familiar) and the student cohorts who actually take the tests are not representative of the population but tend to feature the most economically advantaged. The human cost of these tests is also a cause for concern, with mythical "tiger mothers" demanding nothing less than the best from their put-upon children.

In 2010 I was given a chance to go and see the system for myself when eight schools in our area across all phases were invited to form a partnership with schools in Suzhou, a rapidly expanding city of six million inhabitants two hours west of Shanghai. The Chinese schools we visited in the course of two trips were exceptionally welcoming. I referred earlier to first impressions: we could learn from the Chinese attitude to hospitality. The first thing you see is a personal welcome message on the electronic screen outside the school. A delegation meets you and the tour of the school get underway with a camera crew in tow. Students read from prepared scripts at different stops and then you go to the conference room for tea and often a film prospectus about the school. The classes in a secondary school are large, typically with forty-five to fifty students. The classroom arrangement is formal, with rows of individual desks facing the front. The students tend to stay where they are and the teachers move from lesson to lesson. The pedagogy is highly teacher-led, with rote learning, long hours and a lot of testing. There is not much room for practical experimentation or exploration. You will not see too many science or technology labs. The curriculum is book-based and knowledge-driven. There is no reference, as far as I could see, to the spiritual. This is still after all a Communist country with a materialist world view. There is a good deal of emphasis on virtue, in the tradition of Confucius, but that is not transcendent.

The students learn English from a very early age. They *want* to learn English: more than once we were stopped in the street by groups of students and asked if they could practise their English on us for five minutes. The system is highly competitive, with students ranked for everything. Boards around the schools celebrate the best students, the best classes, the best teachers. There is a completely unembarrassed culture of competition and success. I was shown into a room and introduced to "our six best teachers". The ranking of students determines the next stage of their education, with the top universities taking the top students from across the country. Due to the one-child policy, students are the tip of an inverted pyramid, with the pressure of expectation bearing down from parents, grandparents and even great-grandparents. In the more affluent areas, private tuition is a major industry as parents seek to gain an edge for their children in the tests. There are many signs that we are going in the same direction, but is it the best direction?

Unlike in the west, the Chinese culture is strongly collectivist, with a high regard for authority. In that respect, it is has more in common with the Catholic Church than with liberal democracies. Most of the people you speak to are "on message" and will generally not criticise or question authority. Any discussion about human rights (and any reference to Tiananmen Square) is simply off limits. There is a great deal of enthusiasm for China as a culture, as a nation, as a project. In each school I visited I noticed there was a large open area, with a podium and flagpoles. Most of the secondary schools have between two and three thousand students. They gather in these large open areas at the beginning of the week. The principal sets the tone with inspirational words, the flag is raised and they sing patriotic songs. It is also where they exercise. I arrived one morning at a school and could not see any students. I was aware of a noise, which sounded like distant drumming. We turned the corner and I was amazed to see the entire school, including the teachers, running in class groups around the yard. It was "wake and shake" on a giant scale.

It is only when you scratch the surface, and catch people a little off guard, that they may admit to problems. With a growing economy, the students have a richer diet than their parents and certainly their grandparents. They eat more meat: they are *bigger* than they used to be. Technology has opened them up to a global culture, although you will not see much technology in the classroom. You will see more interactive whiteboards in a British classroom than a Chinese classroom, but mobile phone possession is booming: estimates suggest that around half of the Chinese population (six hundred million people) now own a mobile phone. Despite the nervousness of the authorities, this means that the digital global culture has well and truly arrived. You will see a Premier League football match on almost any screen you pass and MTV is everywhere. This culture generally assumes that self-expression is the norm and this will cause tension in a society where traditionally the self was always at the service of the State.

Teachers will tell you in their more unguarded moments that behaviour is now a bit of a problem. In one school, just down the corridor from the office of the Communist Party representative (every school has one), I noticed a sign (in English) for a Psychological Consulting Room. The bright colours and potted plants inside revealed the purpose of the room: to counsel the anxious or badly behaved – a new phenomenon for the Chinese. The challenge for the authorities is how to balance traditional adherence to central control with the needs of young people who want to express themselves and at the same time are dealing with the intense pressures of a highly competitive educational system. China is a fiercely driven society, with a five-year plan for what needs to be done. When you see the photographs of Shanghai city centre in 1990 compared to 2010, the development in twenty years is staggering. It's like they are doing the industrial revolution and the 1960s on fast forward.

I fully understood that the agenda was shifting when the Chinese teachers and administrators visited us. I showed a group round my school, failing to replicate the great sense of occasion which they generated for me. My secondary school is I'm sure much like most secondary schools: generally polite and well-behaved students, some teacher-led lessons, some group work, personalised working in art, lively role play in drama, choral repetition in languages, peer assessment in PE, well-ordered out-of-the-seat practical experiments in science, and so on. The representative from Suzhou didn't say much on the way round but then later in my office suddenly said, "This is what we need." When I asked him what he meant he explained that in China the next five-year plan was going to see a shift from Made in China to Designed in China and that was not going to happen until the students were able to think for themselves, explore, challenge and create. You could say that they are looking to move from an Enlightenment world view to a Romantic world view. How they manage that change process is their biggest challenge; how well they manage that challenge will have consequences for us all.

There are signs of this shift in other regions. Last year, the *Times Educational Supplement* reported from a seminar in London which was addressed by Professor Lee Sing Kong, director of Singapore's National Institute of Education. His comments showed a remarkable development in thinking from what we consider to be his system's commitment to core knowledge and traditional teaching methods:

We need to go beyond academic education to work on the holistic development of the child. We are emphasising a holistic education rather than one that just emphasises knowledge and skills to create a value-based and student-centric education. We are dealing with twenty-first-century digital learners who have a very different expectation of what learning is about. They prefer learning from their experiences and like to study as a group.[5]

Shift is happening. An emphasis on basic numeracy and literacy will still be a feature of the Singapore system, but there will be a much greater drive for twenty-first-century skills such as team work and "flipped learning", where students use class time to apply knowledge gained from watching online lessons at home. Singapore no longer judges its schools on exam results. According to Professor Lee, "The philosophy of holistic education means we must move away from just academically centred parameters of measurement." I know a number of headteachers who would say Amen to that. Professor Lee has clearly read the script, in fact he sounds like one of the authors. "It is estimated that knowledge will double every two and a half years," he said. "Employers are telling us that they cannot predict what kind of jobs will be available in five years' time."[6]

A Human Ecology

I have no doubt that many leaders in Catholic education will find themselves in agreement with Professor Lee. The holistic development of the child has been a cornerstone of Catholic educational thinking for at least the last six decades. The statement of educational principles from Vatican II stressed that part of the dignity of being a person was an inalienable right to an education in which, "children and young people should be assisted in the harmonious development of their physical, moral and intellectual endowments."[7] As the then Archbishop Vincent Nichols reminded us when he was the chairman of the Catholic Education Service for England and Wales, this line of thinking was taken up and developed by St John Paul II. In the 1995 encyclical, *Evangelium Vitae*, he first coined the evocative phrase "human ecology" to describe the kind of rounded education considered by the Church to be fundamental to the mission of Catholic schools:

An all-round education seeks to develop every aspect of the individual: social, intellectual, emotional, moral and spiritual. For there is an ecology of human growth which means that if any one of these elements is overlooked all the others suffer.[8]

The mission of the school, and the prime purpose of the school leader, is to create an environment, a Gospel-animated climate, where this human ecology can be promoted. In the same article, Archbishop Nichols reminds us that, "In a Catholic school, the true development of the person, pupils and staff, takes precedence over all other things."[9] In other words, Catholic schools should always have at the heart of their educational purpose a philosophy of personalisation, in which the individual young person can grow and mature in a rounded way and discover the unique and original gifts which are part of their calling. This places us very much in the mainstream of progressive educational thinking, as espoused by Ken Robinson, Professor Lee and others. We may differ when it comes to our sources of inspiration, but we are in tune with their vision.

So what does personalisation look like in practice? I think it's worth saying from the outset that it does not mean *individualisation*. There may be some schools where students have an individual timetable and curriculum, supported by a customised IT package, and that may well be the future, but in most schools at the moment that is not possible. What we can do is *personalise the learning* to a significant degree. In fact, it's what any skilled teacher does anyway, but as leaders our job is to look to how we can create and sustain a culture of personalisation across the school; in our case a culture of *Christian personalisation*.

Into the Deeps

Professor David Hargreaves, former Chief Inspector of the Inner London Education Authority and Fellow of Wolfson College, Cambridge, has been one of the leading thinkers on personalisation in education. His early work with the Specialist Schools and Academies Trust (SSAT) developed a framework of nine "gateways" to personalised learning. He arrived at this framework in collaboration with practitioners and it soon became clear to him and the headteachers that nine gateways were too many and

could lead to working in isolated "silos". He then suggested that the nine gateways could be clustered into four "deeps" of personalisation.[10] I immediately took to this thinking, since it resonated so strongly with the metaphorical world of Catholic schools. The original four deeps were as follows:

Deep Learning

This involves a virtuous cycle of *assessment for learning*, with *student voice* at the heart of the learning process and students who have an understanding of *how they learn*. Assessment for learning, developed by Professor Paul Black (*Assessment for Learning: Putting it into Practice*, 2003) and promoted vigorously by Professor Dylan Williams (*Embedded Formative Assessment*, 2011) among others, seeks to personalise learning with high-quality feedback to students about what they need to do to improve based on a detailed knowledge of the assessment objectives. The best practice in assessment allows room for students to respond to the teacher's comments and show their own understanding. The most confident teachers use student voice to help evaluate their practice and co-construct the learning objectives. Students will be able to learn most effectively when they have some understanding of how they learn best and how their young brain works. Deep learning also invites the students to grow into higher-order thinkers. Shallow learning has been a feature in the education system due to the pressure to achieve the magical thresholds of Level 4 or Grade C. For very understandable reasons, schools were tempted to fill students with the shallow learning they needed to achieve these thresholds rather than take the time to develop the deep learning which would better serve the needs of an ecology of human growth.

John West-Burnham further distinguishes between *shallow*, *deep* and then *profound* learning as follows:

Shallow	Deep	Profound
Replication	Understanding	Meaning
Application	Transfer	Creativity
Information	Knowledge	Wisdom
Experience	Reflection	Intuition
Extrinsic	Intrinsic	Moral
Acceptance	Interpretation	Challenge
Dependence	Independence	Interdependence

He is certainly not dismissive of shallow learning, which has a place in the learning process, but the growth to maturity of the individual, in the kind of ways we have been exploring above, requires a journey from shallow to profound learning. West-Burnham compares shallow learning to "tourist" Italian. So, for example, I have enough vocabulary and grammar to survive (I can order a beer and find a room for the night). Deep learning of Italian would allow me to engage in spontaneous and meaningful conversations (I can chat to the waiter about the form of the local football team). Profound learning would mean that not only could I engage meaningfully in the high points of Italian culture but possibly contribute to them (I'm in a heated debate about the merits of Rafael and Michelangelo). He describes profound learning as critical to the growth of the individual:

Profound learning is about the creation of personal meaning and so enhances wisdom and creativity. The motivation to learn is moral and the outcome of profound learning is the ability and willingness to challenge orthodoxy. Such learning is sustained through interdependent engagement in problem-solving and thinking. [11]

We should not assume that this profound learning is reserved for our students in secondary schools or higher education. We consistently underestimate what children in primary schools are capable of and have achieved. Most secondary schools do not pay nearly enough proper attention to transition for learning and a great deal of time is wasted before the students return to the level of learning they enjoyed in Key Stage Two. Nor should we be overly anxious about West-Burnham's call to challenge orthodoxy. Remember what Pope Francis says in "The Joy of the Gospel" about developing critical thinking in our young people, and before that "The Catholic School" insisted on the formation of the pupils' critical faculties. The Church invites our schools to allow young people to engage in profound thinking, to challenge the orthodoxy of the way things are and to consider the radical proposition that the Gospel of Jesus Christ is the way to fullness of life.

The Church has also consistently insisted on wisdom as an aim of the educational process. The most recent document from the Congregation for Catholic Education, "Educating to Intercultural Dialogue in Catholic Schools: Living in Harmony for a Civilization of Love" (hereafter "Educating to Intercultural Dialogue") was published in October

2013 with the approval of Pope Francis. It has been somewhat under the radar since its publication, but it is another excellent document, which looks in particular at the challenges facing Catholic education in a multicultural society. In Chapter Four I referred to the developing consequences of the Trojan Horse controversy. Anyone with any strategic interest in Catholic education will find much guidance in this new document. As far as the climate for learning is concerned, the document reaffirms a long-held Catholic position:

It has been said that we live in a knowledge-based society. However, Catholic schools are encouraged to promote a wisdom-based society, to go beyond knowledge and educate people to think, evaluating facts in the light of values. They educate people to take on responsibility and duties, and exercise active citizenship.[12]

Deep learning, or profound learning as West-Burnham describes it, should always be a feature of the Catholic school.

Deep Support

If students are to engage in deep learning, argues Hargreaves, they will need new forms of enriched support. This deep support will be more personalised and concern itself with the broader well-being of students, including their health, safety, and freedom from poverty and disadvantage. This resonates very strongly with the mission of Catholic schools, especially the emphasis on support for the disadvantaged. Hargreaves, however, keeps taking us back to learning. Supportive general mentoring and

counselling is one thing, and can be critical, but he would rather see a sustained focus on personalised support for learning, in and beyond the classroom, so that all students are enabled to flourish. Ofsted is often critical about how schools use teaching assistants in the classrooms: it is an area in which many schools would seem to require improvement. In terms of the inspiration we have been drawing from the Church, deep support is another way of describing the art of accompaniment which should be a characteristic of the Christian community. As leaders we are constantly challenged to evaluate the effectiveness of that support against our mission principles.

Deep Experience

This "deep" is where leadership must turn its attention to the kind of *curriculum* which engages students with the best use of *new technologies*. Hargreaves reminds us that:

to make the experience of schooling engaging for all students may entail some restructuring, rather than merely tinkering with the curriculum to make it more "relevant" or using the new technologies as decorative modifications to the routine of lessons. Schooling should not be dominated by a curriculum over which students have little ownership and which is delivered to them without the engaging challenges that so many young people crave in the rest of their lives out of school.[13]

Schools have made very good use of the new technologies to offer students personalised learning outside of the classrooms, with skilled use of portals and virtual learning platforms. As an English teacher by trade I have always felt slightly behind the curve in that respect and have relied on the expertise of my colleagues to move us in the right direction. I do believe however that some schools have got it seriously wrong in their evangelical zeal for IT 24/7, as if the world of *Shift Happens* isn't happening quickly enough.

I was once shown round a brand new twenty-five-million-pound school, the type that looks like an airport terminal from a distance, with sliding doors and a cavernous atrium to greet you. The headteacher had worked exceptionally hard on the project and over the years had improved the school from rural dump to a gleaming school of choice for many families for miles around. In the process she had undoubtedly improved the education and life chances of thousands of young people. Her IT strategy, however, left me cold. Every child in the school, she proudly told me, has been given an iPad. This could be seen as a bold step to prepare our students for the world they will face as adults. When we walked round at lunchtime we saw the reality: many students sitting transfixed by their devices, not talking to each other, not running around outside. It struck me that they had probably spent most of their lessons in front of a screen, the same in their breaks, and when they went home they could well be gaming on their computer into the small hours.

This is not what I would call a rounded education, and it's not what the educationalists we have been considering would call a holistic education. A human ecology demands that we pay attention to the healthy growth of all a young person's endowments.

IT has a major part to play in that, but so have a lot of other things. Deep experience can also cover all those other events – cultural, social, sporting – we want our children and young people to experience while they are in our schools. In some cases they *need* to experience them, as we saw in Chapter Four, for any kind of fullness of life.

In a Catholic school, the taught curriculum can never be the student's entire experience. I have spoken to many headteachers who struggle with the dilemma of focusing almost exclusively on the academic so that the students (and the school) will achieve the best results, but this goes against their instinct. They know that deep experience in a Catholic school is much wider and richer than that. "Educating to Intercultural Dialogue" has the following encouragement for us:

Moreover, given schools' attention to the whole person and to all human experience, they do not limit their responsibilities to the merely didactic. Schools also care for many other aspects of the students' lives, in informal ways (parties, fun moments, etc.), formal ways (presentations from informed guest speakers, discussion times, etc.) and religious experiences (times for liturgy and spirituality, etc.)[14]

In Chapter Two I drew attention to the work of Fr Christopher Jamison OSB, the National Director for Vocation, who has encouraged Catholic schools to consider placing a culture of vocation at the heart of the curriculum. We are not here reverting to any narrow definition of a Catholic curriculum. The

Church in its publications has always understood and respected the integrity of subject disciplines and has never promoted a fundamentalist approach to knowledge. But the Church is also clear that the curriculum and teaching are not neutral and in a Catholic school should be animated by Gospel values. In the years ahead, we will be called to give an account of the purpose of our schools and we must be ready with the answer. In our schools, the curriculum, the deep experience we offer our children and young people, is designed to make them more human, more open to life, love and service, not to indoctrinate or to follow a narrow faith-based agenda, which would provide easy pickings for our opponents.

Deep Leadership

For Hargreaves, deep leadership is required to ensure that deep experience and deep support are implemented in schools so that deep learning takes place. Deep leadership is that which is necessary to create a climate of personalisation in school. It should be stressed in our context that leadership should be seen as a shared enterprise between the headteacher and the governing body, albeit with different core functions (see the DFE's *Governors' Handbook* and more detailed treatment in our sibling book by Sister Judith Russi). I would also consider that deep leadership requires reflection, or in the phrase used by Michael Fullan, slow thinking, which the senior team and governors should find time for together (for more on this see Chapter Seven). Deep leadership does not respond in a panic to the latest short-term plans sent down the line by short-term-thinking politicians. Deep leadership is inspired by moral and spiritual purpose. Deep leadership deepens over the

years: leaders need to be learners and have the humility to learn from everybody. Then the school will enjoy the fruits of their maturity.

In the context of a Catholic school, such deep leadership, as we have explored in an earlier chapter, must involve the depth of personal faith commitment, otherwise you are building your house on sand. As one headteacher put it to me, headship was an authentic expression of who he was. It is more than a job, it is the current manifestation of the vocation to love and service of the disciple, using his or her gifts to the full. And it is a risk. It was risk for St Peter when Jesus asked him to "put out into the deep" (Luke 5:4).

In my school, we adopted the four deeps of personalisation as the four main headings or chapters of our school development plan and found that it helped to give a greater coherence to our intentions. We interpreted personalisation as being at the heart of our mission as a Catholic school to promote the formation of our young people, to celebrate their uniqueness, to give them as much support as we could muster in an experience of school which was as rich and engaging as possible, and to leave us with some notion of what their gifts were calling them to be in the society they were about to enter as young adults. But the four didn't quite do it for us. We ended up adding two more, which we felt expressed the fullest dimension of our work as a Catholic school.

Deep Spiritual Life

We used to have a separate Spiritual Development Plan, which always seemed like something of an add-on, rather than central to our purpose. Thinking in terms of the deeps, it seemed a natural step for us to introduce "deep spiritual life" as a heading in the SDP and then we quickly realised that it was the central deep, the "deep of deeps". I was interested to see that David Hargreaves introduced a fifth deep which he called "deep happiness", which I suppose is a secular version of our deep spiritual life. This deep helped us to fully articulate our purpose. The actions which flowed from it were at the heart of our mission: involving more students in chaplaincy, preparing a mission week, improving the quality of liturgy and assemblies, developing the prayer life of the school. It was also evident that this new deep actually *fed* the others and was enhanced by them. If the content of an individual's treasure box is what educates their heart, then the same is true for an institution: what is in the school's treasure box, what is the most important thing?

The promotion of a deep Christian spiritual life in the school inspired our aspiration for as much deep support as possible for our students. Deep spiritual life should also be a feature of the kind of deep experience of school which would keep the students engaged and motivated and result in the kind of deep learning which encouraged them to think of themselves as children of God called to a higher end. All of this was made possible by deep and reflective leadership at every level. Faculty development plans used the same headings, which mean that deep spiritual life had to figure as central to their thinking. When faculties had their meetings I invited colleagues to construct their agenda under the headings of the deeps. As an idea it found its way into the irrigation system of the school. When I suggested it was perhaps time to leave the deeps, think of another framework, the senior team were

not having it – they liked their deeps. I was struck when we were conducting internal interviews for heads of year how much the language of deep support featured in the thinking of the applicants.

Our final deep sprang from the realisation that we could not provide all the personalised learning on our own. We needed other institutions and the thinking of other colleagues to help us to provide the kind of breadth of deep experience and quality of deep support we wanted for our students. Partnership is also critical to help a school formulate its strategic thinking. So the sixth and (so far) final deep was created: "deep partnerships".

Deep Partnerships

I have come to the view that one of the most important ways in which Catholic schools can meet the challenge of what lies in wait is to form partnerships with other Catholic schools. We will all have a number of overlapping partnerships with a range of other agencies and schools and they will no doubt serve us well, but we will have only mission purpose in common with other Catholic schools. We have seen a dramatic growth in recent years, encouraged by government, of clusters and federations between schools of different kinds. There is a view that the schools of tomorrow will not survive unless they are in a federation of some kind. I have been involved in several, but for me the most fruitful has been the "soft" federation, technically a collaboration, between my school, our eight partner primary schools and the three Catholic independent schools in our area. We have developed a structure with an "executive meeting" of the headteachers six times a year and the "strategic board" of heads and chairs of governing bodies three times a years. The schools all subscribe to a levy to allow the heads to meet in a professional and attractive venue off-site for two to three hours ending with lunch. It may seem indulgent, and it may not survive the challenge of Pope Francis, but when we met in each other's schools the level of distraction did not allow for much work or reflection, especially from our host.

The agenda is drawn up in advance after consultation and the meetings are professionally minuted, which is key. The group is only three years old and there is still much to do but a very clear and purposeful agenda has developed around what we have in common. We have supported each other with leadership briefings and updates, including the sharing of best practice in self-evaluation and Ofsted preparation. We have provided informal mentoring for new heads and worked with each other on the possibility of academy conversion and whether or not this is the best option for us (at the time of writing the State schools in our partnerships are still maintained). We have focused on the teaching of RE in our schools and how to develop a coherent Relationships Education Policy from Year R to Year Thirteen. We have organised an annual Saturday morning conference for heads and chairs of governors with a single thematic focus. Our last conference looked at "New Vocations" in preparation for our diocese's Year of Vocation. We continue to consider how our schools can work together to build and promote a culture of vocations. As I mentioned in Chapter Eight, we have developed our prayer life together by introducing *Lectio Divina* before our meetings.

Some of our most memorable work has involved the children and students. We're always mindful of this question: "How is all this benefiting them?" At the beginning of every school year we now have a federation Mass which brings together students from all our schools in a wonderful eucharistic act of thanksgiving. For the last two years we have held a join "mufti" fundraiser on CAFOD's Fast Day in Lent. Last year a film crew managed to visit every school in the partnership during Fast Day and produce an inspirational film to encourage our future efforts. For Transfer Day we have developed a liturgy involving the headteachers from the partner schools. They "hand over" their children to me in a simple but very moving ceremony. The primary school headteachers publicly ask me to look after their children and the Year Six children ask our Year Ten students to welcome and look after them. We reply that we will and we offer each other a sign of peace over an open Bible, a symbol of what binds us together. Not all the students coming into Year Seven are from our partner schools. With the removal of denominational transport subsidies, the percentage of Catholic children joining us has fallen to around sixty-five per cent, but it is still a very powerful induction for those children who are not from a Catholic background to see how seriously we take their care.

There is no getting away from the fact that there is a sense of underlying competition between my school and the independent schools, but that does not prevent us working together very effectively. The diocese asked us if the independent schools could join our federation when the partnership groupings were being reviewed. We were very happy to welcome our colleagues from the independent sector and have learned a great deal from them and how they run their schools. The Church does not distinguish between types of Catholic school: the mission and expectation remain the same.

There are other schools and colleges we work with to try to provide the most personalised learning we can for our students. It has become more difficult for average-sized secondary schools (my school, with a new sixth form, is growing to around a thousand students) to provide the fullest range of subjects and experiences which students would benefit from. It has also been more challenging to find good partners who are collaboratively minded. In the last few years I have noticed a distinct weakening in the culture of collaboration in the wider school community. If schools are in an academy chain or trust, they very often work within the confines of that arrangement, often to the detriment of wider partnerships. I am not suggesting that Catholic schools should set up similarly closed circles, since that would be fundamentally against our commitment to the common good. I am saying that in order to help us meet what lies in wait with confidence we must work together to support each other and to build the capacity of our schools, in whatever structures best suit local circumstances.

Give to Caesar

A common concern among headteachers when considering innovation of any kind, is to ask how it would help them in an Ofsted inspection. Sadly many headteachers have given up on progressive thinking because they feel it would do them no good in the "bottom line" equation of the Ofsted judgement. I

fully understand this. It would be a brave or perhaps foolish headteacher who ignored Ofsted. But I have never seen much point in Ofsted-bashing. Most of us are State schools, funded by the taxpayers, and the State (Caesar: the secular power), in partnership with the Church, has every right to set out what it expects from us and to ensure that we are delivering. I know that some colleagues have had very stressful experiences of the inspection process and that is perhaps why, at the time of writing, Ofsted will take control of the inspection process back from third-party contractors. But generally we have enjoyed a mutually beneficial partnership with the State, especially since the landmark 1944 Education Act. I would like to look briefly at the State's expectations, as set out in the Ofsted framework, and see if there is any encouragement there for Catholic schools committed to a holistic vision of personalised education.

The purpose of an Ofsted inspection is to judge the quality of education provided in the school. In order to make that judgement the inspectors must first make four key judgements: the achievement of pupils at the school; the quality of teaching in the school; the behaviour and safety of pupils at the school; the quality of leadership in, and management of, the school (including, and increasingly, governance). The criteria for each of these judgements are clearly set out in the *School Inspection Handbook*.[15]

In addition to the four key judgements above inspectors must also consider:

- The spiritual, moral, social, and cultural development of pupils at the school.

- The extent to which the education provided by the school meets the needs of the range of pupils at the school, and in particular the needs of pupils who have a disability, for the purposes of the Equality Act 2010, and pupils who have special educational needs.

When the Education Reform Act of 1988 was published it was noted with satisfaction by many in the Church that, after a great deal of effective lobbying, the purpose of an education was described as being to provide a balanced and broadly based curriculum which, "promotes the *spiritual* [my emphasis], moral, cultural, mental and physical development of the pupils; and prepares such pupils for the opportunities, responsibilities and experiences of adult life."[16] This formulation has never been repealed in subsequent acts and amendments. The State, then, promotes a rounded or holistic view of education. The State also says that in the first instance schools should promote the spiritual development of their pupils.

It is interesting to see how much guidance has been produced by Ofsted and others on how to teach, how to ensure good behaviour, how to lead and manage, compared to how much has been produced on promoting the spiritual development of pupils. The reality is that the State finds itself in a spot of bother when it comes to matters spiritual. It does not want to offend anyone with the wrong kind of talk about transcendent things, but there it is in the opening lines of the most significant reform act since the Second World War. The last major report from Ofsted on SMSC was published in 2004: "Promoting and Evaluating Pupils' Spiritual, Moral, Social and Cultural Development". The document is full of references to what had been up until that point a sustained engagement with what these categories meant. It talks about, "awe, wonder and mystery – being inspired by the natural world, mystery or human achievement."[17] The language over the subsequent ten years has become progressively more functional and tentative. The April 2014 handbook asked inspectors to look for evidence that the students are, "reflective about beliefs, values and more profound aspects of human experience," and "develop awareness of and respect for diversity in relation to, for example, gender, race, religion and belief, culture, sexual orientation and disability."[18] It is all entirely laudable, but the colour and poetry has been drained out of the language. The transcendent has been flattened.

Since the Trojan Horse controversy in 2014 (see Chapter Four) the *School Inspection Handbook* has been revised again (July 2014) and the section defining spiritual, moral, social and cultural development has changed in very significant ways. There is an explicit focus on promoting British values as a response to the concern that those values were being undermined by a small number of community schools which sought to radicalise its pupils. There is a reference to "respect for the civil and criminal law of England" and an encouragement for pupils to offer, "reasoned views about moral and ethical issues."[19] I think we could be in contentious territory here. This is the language of the Enlightenment, the period of intellectual revolution in Europe when reason was promoted as the great defence against the irrational and superstitious, as supposedly embodied in particular in the Catholic faith.

The section on the "Quality of leadership in and management of the school" has been significantly enlarged to address the new concerns of the State regarding radical extreme Islamic views being promoted in schools. There is a far greater emphasis on the role of the governing body, no doubt in part because in the Trojan Horse controversy it was apparently governors who were leading the radicalisation agenda. Governors are expected to ensure that the school promotes, "tolerance of and respect for people of all faiths (or those of no faith), cultures and lifestyles."[20] In that one word "lifestyles" there could be any number of challenges for Catholic schools. This is why we require deep leadership, because we will need wisdom to implement the revised expectations of the State while still being true to our mission.

We need to join this debate and make the case in the public square that our religion promotes human flourishing. We cannot allow the more aggressive secular groups to confuse us with the forces of extremism which are regarded as a threat to the very existence of our society. You can see how the secularists are only one step away from demanding a continental system where State-provided education has no Church involvement. We have a case to make and we need not sound defensive. Our schools and colleges are vibrant, successful and well regarded by many in the political and educational establishment, although we cannot take that for granted. Our voice needs to be heard. The richness of our mission needs to be made clear to as wide an audience as possible.

Outstanding/Distinguished

With regards to the Ofsted criteria for an "outstanding" grade for overall effectiveness, the July 2014 handbook is very similar to previous versions, apart from a new emphasis on a "broad and balanced" curriculum (in response to fears of a narrowly religious curriculum) and the "most able" (which does not always sit entirely comfortably with our mission). We should also bear in mind that if any of the four key judgements (for example leadership and management) are "requires improvement", then the overall judgement is likely to be "requires improvement". In the criteria for "outstanding", we will recognise many of the terms and concepts we have been exploring in this study:

- Teaching is outstanding and, together with a rich, relevant, broad and balanced curriculum, contributes to outstanding learning and achievement, significant growth in pupils' knowledge and excellent attitudes to learning.

- Pupils, and particular groups of pupils, have excellent educational experiences at school and these ensure that they are very well equipped for the next stage of their education, training or employment.

- There is excellent practice that ensures that all pupils have high levels of literacy and mathematical knowledge, understanding and skills appropriate to their age.

- The school's practice consistently reflects the highest expectations of staff and the highest aspirations for pupils, including the most able, disabled pupils and those with special educational needs.

• Best practice is spread effectively in a drive for continuous improvement.

• The school's thoughtful and wide-ranging promotion of pupils' spiritual, moral, social and cultural development and their physical well-being enables them to thrive in a supportive, highly cohesive learning community.

School Inspection Handbook, July 2014

Overall, it is what we aspire to, since the Church expects all Catholic schools to be at least as "distinguished" as other schools in the area. There is nothing in that list which is alien to the mission of a Catholic school (provided a focus on the "most able" does not distract us from the needs of the least able and most vulnerable). We certainly consider our mission to consist of more than that but, as a circle within a circle, we can and should embrace all of the above.

It is also worth commenting finally on the development of thinking from Ofsted with regards to the quality of teaching. It has been made very clear by Her Majesty's Chief Inspector that the age of a desired methodology in the classroom is well and truly over. Ofsted is now only interested in the *impact* of the teaching. Whatever method you use is not the point. The key question for the teacher is now: "What is the impact of what you are doing on the children and students in front of you? When they leave the room an hour from now, what do they

know that they did not know before, how do you know what they know, and in what kind of climate or atmosphere have they learned?" I think we should regard this as a liberation. It should give us complete confidence to adopt the personalised practices of assessment for learning (or whatever other methodology we consider appropriate) provided they have an impact. It seems to me that we are uniquely placed in our schools to develop a Catholic pedagogy fit for the twenty-first century which will serve our students well, whatever lies in wait.

[1] *Evangelii Gaudium*, 263.
[2] K. Robinson, *Out of Our Minds* (Chichester: Capstone Publishing, 2011), p. 15.
[3] Ibid., p. 269.
[4] Department for Education and Skills, *Personalised Learning: Building a New Relationship with Schools* (DfES 2004). Found at: http://webarchive.nationalarchives.gov.uk/20130401151715/http://www.education.gov.uk/publications/standard/publicationDetail/Page1/PERSONAL-LEARNING
[5] W. Stewart, "Singapore heads in a bold new direction", *Times Educational Supplement* (20 September 2013).
[6] Ibid.
[7] "Educational Guidance in Human Love", 19. Found at: www.vatican.va
[8] Cited in Cardinal Vincent Nichols, "Leading a Catholic school", from *Visions for Leadership* (London: Heythrop Institute for Religion, Ethics and Public Life, 2009).
[9] Ibid., p. 30.
[10] D. Hargreaves, *A New Shape for Schooling?* (London: Specialist Schools and Academies Trust, 2006).
[11] J. West-Burnham, "Learning to lead", from *Handbook of Educational Leadership and Management* (London: Pearson Education, 2003), p. 55.
[12] Congregation for Catholic Education, "Educating to Intercultural Dialogue in Catholic Schools: Living in Harmony for a Civilization of Love" (2013), 66.
[13] Hargreaves, 2006, p. 8.
[14] Congregation for Catholic Education, 2013, 63.
[15] Ofsted, *School Inspection Handbook* (Ofsted, July 2014). Found at: http://www.ofsted.gov.uk/resources/school-inspection-handbook
[16] Education Reform Act 1988. Found at: http://www.legislation.gov.uk/ukpga/1988/40/contents
[17] Ofsted, "Promoting and Evaluating Pupils' Spiritual, Moral, Social and Cultural Development" (Ofsted, 2004), p. 9.
[18] Ofsted, *School Inspection Handbook* (Ofsted, April 2014, no longer available).
[19] Ofsted, 2014.
[20] Ibid., p. 47.

CHAPTER 10

A Framework for Catholic Schools in the Twenty-first Century

My final task is to try and bring together some of my main observations and to begin a discussion on a possible new framework for our schools in the twenty-first century. This framework is merely the fruits of my own reflection. It is not the outcome of a long and rigorous process of academic review and is no doubt flawed as a result. It may help to prompt us in the right direction.

The term "3G" is short for the "third generation" of mobile telecommunications technology. A new generation of cellular standards has appeared about every ten years since 1G in 1981/1982. Now 4G is upon us, with ever greater frequency bands and data rates (whatever that means). I thought it might be helpful, therefore, to commandeer the language of shifting technology for an understanding of what we need to focus on to be schools true to our mission and fit for the demands of the twenty-first century. The 4Gs I am proposing for a new framework for Catholic schools are as follows:

GOSPEL	GROWTH
GLOBAL	GOOD TO GREAT

Gospel

Catholic schools should always be Gospel schools. That means they should be mindful to implement all of the Church's expectations for its schools, to ensure that Christ is the foundation of the educational enterprise, that Gospel values inform and inspire all that we do and that this results in a climate which is animated by the Gospel. These days we have been called back to the radiance of the Gospel with renewed fervour, called to a mission renewal. Catholic schools will always teach the Deposit of Faith, but that is more about knowledge. The Big Gospel is an invitation to life and transformation.

Scholars for example will tell us that the best translation of the Greek word used to describe the first call of Jesus to his disciples – *metanoia* – is not so much "repent", but "change your thinking". It is harder than repent, which is something we can easily sign up to and then fall back later. To change the way you think about your life, to alter your basic perception, is more like cognitive surgery, but that is what Jesus wants. He is rewriting conventional wisdom – *but I say this to you* – and "None of the rulers of this age understood this; for if they had, they would not have crucified the Lord of glory" (1

Corinthians 2:8). To what extent do our schools promote the counter-cultural wisdom of Jesus?

Richard Rohr tells us that two thirds of the teaching of Jesus is about compassion, forgiveness and reconciliation. Forgiveness lies at the very heart of the identity of God. How long have we laboured under quite a different perception? One of the most memorable images Jesus gives us of God is an ungainly father running out to embrace his returned son before he even asks for forgiveness. Jesus does not seem to worry about preconditions for forgiveness. It's freely given and that's what transforms people. That's why the woman gatecrashed Simon the Pharisee's dinner party: she showed great love *because* she had been forgiven, not the other way round (Luke 7:36-50).

On the cross, Jesus does not just forgive the little cohort of humanity in front of him, he reconciles us all to God, *he forgives reality*. He suffers the worst the human condition can inflict on another human being and does not throw it back, but absorbs it and transforms it in glory. And what happens when the risen Jesus appears before the men who ran away from him at his hour of great need? *He doesn't even mention it*. As Rohr says, in the risen Christ we have an icon of God whose very breath is forgiveness. No violence, no revenge, no conditions. Is this radical forgiveness a reality in our schools?

We are the only major world religion which worships the victim – the naked criminal crucified outside of the city walls by the State, a problem tidied up by the fretful and scheming authorities. This is the one we call Lord. Jesus is an unlikely candidate for God. Such

a God should also make us forever suspicious about all uses of power over other people. Look at what Jesus does: he heals and empowers, he looks lovingly, he does not dominate, humiliate, or demean.

Listen to his teaching. His preferred pedagogy was the parable: story, invitation, challenge, simile, imagination – not binary rules and regulations. Rohr tells us that we have spent hundreds of years as a Church assuming that human beings are very simple and we have to make the law very complex to cover every possible situation. There was good reason for this. But Jesus seems to work the other way round: he regards people as complex with all their stories and ailments but he makes it very simple for them – love God, love your neighbour, you're forgiven, go in peace. They don't have to sign up to anything, just go in peace. The membership requirements and the numbers game come later, maybe they have to, but Jesus just keeps moving, driven by mission, not bothered by numbers.

Jesus uses images all the time of smallness, slow growth, hiddenness. He mocks those who crave attention and who worry about their status and their clothes. "If Jesus is the revelation of what is going on inside the mind of God (Colossians 1:15)," observes Rohr, "which is the core of the Christian faith, then we are forced to conclude that God is very humble."[1] This is a God and a Gospel that the young people of today can relate to. They are not attracted to authority figures or the heroes of previous generations. Those statues have toppled. If we are to give them an alternative to the celebrities who demand so much of their time, we need to bring them this Jesus, who always enters history on a donkey. I was inspired by one primary headteacher whose assembly every Monday morning was the Gospel of the day before. He knew that most of his children had not been to Mass and saw it as his duty to bring the Gospel to them.

Are our schools *Gospel schools*? Let us develop an understanding of what that might mean. A Gospel school will of course meet all the orthodox expectations of the Church, all the existing frameworks, and respond with imagination and energy to the call of Francis to return to the source, to see it in new and inspiring ways.

Growth

Catholic schools should be schools of growth or formation for our children, students and staff, *health centres of the spirit*, as I heard one colleague say. Jesus came to bring fullness of life to people, and that is what we are called to do in our schools. The Church has consistently asked us to focus on the promotion of the person, to help them to discover the "original gift" and to come to some understanding of what God's dream is for them. We have been provided by the Church with an inspiring document which will help us to *build cultures of vocation* in our schools. I have to acknowledge that, of all the school leaders I spoke to, nobody had read "New Vocations". It was clear that there was some interest in the notion of vocation in schools, but it mostly centred around being the best you can be, and for schools in more deprived communities there was a very understandable emphasis on aspiration for their students.

Building a culture of vocation is mostly one bullet point in the many diocesan programmes around the country. It should take priority because it is no less than an invitation from the Church to accompany our young people in their formative years in a world which is over-stimulated and highly complex. We are invited to share with them the treasures of the faith in ways that will make sense to them and to help them to see that their life has a great purpose and great worth.

The idea of "human ecology" means that we want our young people to grow as rounded individuals. We do that well in our schools. We are as committed as any other type of school to the academic achievement of our students and we understand the need for that as part of our mission. We have a particular care for the growth and achievement of our most vulnerable students, since in the Gospels Jesus showed an exceptional interest in the lost, the least of these, the one cast out by the community.

Global

The Roman Catholic Church has always been trans-national but for a very long time was Euro-centric, or more specifically Roman. Vatican II opened the Church up to the concerns of the whole human family and now, with the pontificate of Francis, we have a renewed global perspective. The Church has consistently called us to be attentive to the common good, the needs of our brothers and sisters who are deprived of the dignity of a life without poverty. There is a great danger in school that our engagement with poverty ends after the assembly and the "mufti" fundraiser. We are called upon to transform society, to do something.

In Manila, the staff and students St Scholastica's will march on the streets protesting against corruption. They do not have a shadow of a doubt that this is the purpose of their Catholic school. I for one feel very timid in comparison. I wasn't very comfortable getting some placards together for the debate in the council chambers about denominational transport. But we have always been called to promote the common good. The social teaching of the Church should find a home in our curriculum. As I mentioned earlier, I know of one diocese where the bishop has asked for a continuous programme to deliver the main elements of this teaching from Key Stages One to Five.

The statistics of *Shift Happens* (see Chapter Nine) are compelling but for Catholic schools there is another set of observations which should inspire our work to improve the conditions for our brothers and sisters. CAFOD has been a wonderful resource over the years and has always prompted us to consider the painful realities of our world and as Christians do something about the fact that:

- 50,000 people die every day as a result of poverty.

- 2.6 billion do not have access to basic sanitation, including toilets.

- 69 million primary-school aged children don't go to school.

- 783 million people don't have access to safe drinking water.

- About 14.9 million children in sub-Saharan Africa have lost one or both parents because of AIDS.

- The chance of a woman dying in pregnancy in sub-Saharan Africa is one in 30; in the developed world it is one in 5,600.[2]

The other aspect of a global perspective which demands our attention, and which is rumoured to be the subject of the next encyclical from Pope Francis, is climate change and its devastating impact on the poorest communities. In the Church we have seen a distinct shift away from a focus on personal piety to a consideration of the needs of our brothers and sisters in the wider community. "Educating to Intercultural Dialogue" sums up the implications for Catholic schools thus:

The curriculum must help the students reflect on the great problems of our time, including those where one sees more clearly the difficult situation of a large part of humanity's living conditions. These would include the unequal distribution of resources, poverty, injustice and human rights denied. "Poverty" implies a careful consideration of the phenomenon of globalization, and suggests a broad and developed vision of poverty, in all its various forms and causes.[3]

Catholic schools should be global in their outlook but they should also, as Francis reminds us, be *grounded*. We should never forget what is going on in or own community, which is often harder to see. I was very struck during one visit to a school when the headteacher told me about the local scandal of "beds in sheds". The area looked for the most part to be full of well-maintained residential properties, but behind that façade respectable people were letting out their garden sheds to migrant workers for exorbitant rents. The sheds had no heating, lighting or sanitation, just the warmth of bodies. The headteacher showed me a "heat map" of the area taken from the air at night: almost every property had a glow at the bottom of the garden, human beings huddled up among the gardening tools. The statistics for child poverty in this country are also shocking: on average throughout England, over one in five (21.3 per cent) children are classified as below the poverty line. In some areas of our large cities, this rises to over half. In terms of numbers this means that 2.5 million children live below the poverty line in this country. The figure has improved considerably since 1998/1999 when it was 3.4 million but it is still a scandalous figure.[4]

Schools will be located in very different communities throughout the country. My own school is in a small city which on the face of it is wealthy, but there are pockets of severe deprivation. I have always felt that it was important that our "home" charity was the local shelter for homeless people, since it is easy to forget that amidst such seeming affluence there is still such a problem. Many schools, especially in the urban centres, have signed up to the living wage campaign (**www.livingwage.org.uk**) to lead by example and ensure that their own employees are paid a living wage. The current living wage for London is £8.80 and for outside of London it is £7.65 per hour. This figure is reviewed and set annually by the Centre for Research in Social Policy at Loughborough University. You will see on some school websites a commitment to be a Living Wage Employer.

Many of our schools have well-established links with schools and projects in other countries, often through the global networks of Catholic agencies. Our schools are naturally inclined to be outward-facing international schools and much of the current curriculum supports that outlook (unless the politicians decide we need to be more parochial). For our schools, there is profoundly moral dimension to these partnerships. As Christians we have a foundational belief in the "sacred grandeur" of all our brothers and sisters. At a time when racism is on the increase in our country we have an important role as witnesses to the dignity of all people. It is important that we promote this relentlessly in our schools and that our policies (above all practices in promoting race equality) are best practice.

Good to Great

To face the challenges of this century our schools will need above all great leadership. I don't mean great in any worldly sense, although our leaders will share many of the qualities of great secular leaders. When Jesus was faced with the naked leadership ambition of some of his disciples he told them that, "whoever wishes to become great among you must be your servant" (Mark 10:43). We may need more support from our theologians to help us understand the theology of servant leadership but as practical theologians inspired by the example of Pope Francis we have an intuitive grasp of what is involved. It is also encouraging to discover that this kind of egoless leadership is fit for purpose in the culture of change. As we saw in Chapter Six, the research of Jim Collins concluded that the most effective leaders in the business world had the same characteristics in common: humility and will.

Michael Fullan, in his research, proposed that there were five components to effective leadership in a culture of change:

The conclusion then is that leaders will increase their effectiveness if they continually work on the five components of leadership – if they pursue moral purpose, understand the change process, develop relationships, foster knowledge building, and strive for coherence – with energy, enthusiasm, and hopefulness.[5]

Fullan reminds us of the importance of deploying the most appropriate leadership styles as a prerequisite for understanding the change process. Headteachers will have an instinctive grasp of the styles of leadership required depending on the context of their school. As one headteacher told me he uses several different styles in one day, but the generally recognised main leadership styles are the ones identified by Daniel Goleman as:

• Coercive – the leader demands compliance ("Do what I tell you").

• Authoritative – the leader mobilises people towards a vision ("Come with me").

• Affiliative – the leader creates harmony and builds emotional bonds ("People come first").

• Democratic – the leader forges consensus through participation.

• Pacesetting – the leader sets high standards for performance ("Do as I do, now").

• Coaching – the leader develops people for the future ("Try this").[6]

Two of the six styles have been found to have a consistently negative impact on climate and in turn performance: *coercive* and *pacesetting*. The danger in coercive is that people resent and resist. It can be tempting in a school setting when there is an urgent need for a turnaround, but you've still got to take people with you. The pacesetting style can often lead to people being overwhelmed and burning out. We have examined the importance of *koinonia*, or community, in a Catholic school. Circumstances do very enormously but I would have thought that in most Catholic schools leadership at all levels should be deploying a range of authoritative, affiliative, democratic and coaching styles.

We also need leaders who are self-aware, who have high levels of what Goleman calls "emotional intelligence", who have a sensible approach to work/life balance and a hinterland to retire to in order to refresh themselves. But above all we need headteachers who have a spiritual life and are motivated by a missionary heart, who see themselves as disciples first and foremost with a vocation which at this moment in time means being a headteacher or leader in a Catholic school. We need headteachers who pray and who have the confidence to teach others how to pray and to lead their school communities in prayer.

As Catholic headteachers we are expected to deliver everything that our colleagues in the non-faith sector are expected to deliver and more. There is a wealth of literature and support for the leadership skills and competencies required to run a school. The purpose of this book has not been to attempt a review of that literature or even to contribute to that thinking, but rather to try and offer some fresh thinking which will support our colleagues in their focus on mission integrity and to survive and thrive in the process. It has been a rare privilege to visit so many Catholic schools and speak to so many great leaders and wonderful students. I can only conclude that our sector is in very good shape. Our data in terms of results and Ofsted inspections are above national averages (and that helps enormously when anybody begins to question our existence), but more than that we seem to have a cohort of leaders at the moment who are more than capable of leading our schools into the twenty-first century and provide for our young people the kind of education they will need to flourish in the complex and demanding world they will face as adults.

Our sector however is not without its challenges. Society is changing rapidly and the place of religion is under intense scrutiny. The Church in the west is undergoing a crisis of transmission which means that our young people are not being brought up in the same Catholic culture as their parents and grandparents. It means that the teachers and support staff in our schools do not have the same knowledge of Catholic culture as previous generations. I did not detect any such crisis in the current crop of leaders, but the figures show and experience tells us that fewer and fewer colleagues are applying for Catholic

headship and those in the future who do will not have come out of the strong, vibrant, and supportive Catholic communities that formed us. I would therefore like to end by suggesting that as a community we focus all our efforts on the following challenges:

- The creation of a *school of formation* for Catholic headteachers, aspiring headteachers and governors – real or virtual, but preferably real – which nourishes and forms the next generation of Catholic school leaders, with an emphasis on prayer, scripture, spirituality and well-being. This is not new. I have met retired Catholic headteachers who have been calling for such a provision for years, but the call now needs to be more urgent. If we do not attend to this then future generations of Catholic leaders will not have the spiritual life, resources, or personal motivation to interpret the tradition or bring the Gospel to our young people in engaging and convincing ways.

- A national focus on the *formation of our staff*. This is skilled work, since we are not working with the same level of personal faith commitment which we can assume from our leaders, but the people who work in our schools – teachers and support staff – want to be there and want to know more about the extraordinarily rich culture their school is part of. They don't need to write essays about it but they need to know a lot more than they do now. The Catholic Certificate in Religious studies (CCRS) has served a small number of our staff well, but we need more of an "entry-level" or *kerygma* programme for those who are starting from scratch. *How to Survive Working in a Catholic School* (Redemptorist Publications, 2013) was an attempt to meet that need, and it would be even better if a programme was promoted as part of a coherent national strategy.

- We have benefited over the years from a number of national organisations which have endeavoured to support Catholic teachers and leaders in their work, most recently the Catholic Association of Teachers, School and Colleges (CATSC). However we must continually ask ourselves, "Do we have enough opportunities as Catholic leaders in education to meet and communicate with each other on matters of professional interest, including a webforum for discussion of particular topics, a focus on the dissemination of leadership thinking and best practice, the dissemination of Church documents, and the development of Catholic pedagogy?"

- A nationally coordinated effort to *build a culture of vocation* in our schools as outlined in "New Vocations for a New Europe". We need a national vocations framework for schools and the sharing of best practice.

- The urgent need for a *national review* of our purpose and role in society, an answer to the call of Francis for mission renewal. This again is not a new call although it should be given fresh impetus by "The Joy of the Gospel". A letter by Jim Madden, a much-respected retired Catholic headteacher, published in *The Tablet* in 2007, expressed grave concern at the lack of Catholic headteachers coming through to take up new

posts and the lack of a coherent strategy for the formation of Catholic leaders:

We are entitled to hope that this issue will be discussed at the Bishops' Low Week meeting. They might consider a full-scale strategic review of the school system similar to Lord Dearing's for the Church of England in 2000. His report, The Way Ahead, celebrates the achievements of church schools, sets out a vision for their future and gives the Church a coherent national policy. The issue facing Catholic schools are sufficiently weighty to warrant a similar consultation in which all the stakeholders… are represented, and through which our way ahead may be discerned under the guidance of the Spirit.[7]

Whatever lies in wait, we must ensure that we are always ready to give an answer to anyone who demands an account of the hope that is in us (1 Peter 3:15).

[1] R. Rohr with J. Feister, *Jesus' Plan for a New World* (Cincinnati: St Anthony Messenger Press, 1996), p. 137.

[2] Presentation on CAFOD (**www.cafod.org.uk**), with acknowledged sources including the Millennium Development Report 2010.

[3] Congregation for Catholic Education, "Educating to Intercultural Dialogue", 66.

[4] Centre for Research in Social Policy, Loughborough University, *End Child Poverty* (London: Child Poverty Action Group, 2011).

[5] M. Fullan, *Leading in a Culture of Change* (San Francisco: Jossey-Bass, 2001), p. 11.

[6] Cited in Fullan, 2001.

[7] J. Madden, letter published in *The Tablet* (20 January 2007).

FURTHER READING

In addition to the books and documents in the footnotes, here are some suggestions for further reading to support and inspire Catholic leaders:

Brighouse, T. & Woods, D., *The A-Z of School Improvement* (London: Bloomsbury Education, 2013).

Fedduccia, R. Jr SJ (ed.), *Great Catholic Writing: Thought, Literature, Spirituality, Social Action* (Winona: St Mary's Press, 2006).

Gardner, H., *Five Minds for the Future* (Boston: Harvard Business Press, 2008).

Groome, T., *Educating for Life: A Spiritual Vision for Every Teacher and Parent* (Allen: Thomas More, 1998).

Handy, C., *The Hungry Spirit: New Thinking for a New World* (London: Arrow, 2002).

Jamison, C. OSB, *The Disciples' Call: Theologies of Vocation from Scripture to the Present Day* (London: Bloomsbury, 2013).

Jamison, C. OSB, *Finding Sanctuary: Monastic Steps for Everyday Life* (London: Phoenix, 2006).

McBride, D. C.Ss.R., *Waiting on God* (Chawton: Redemptorist, 2003).

Morris A. B., *Fifty Years On: The Case for Catholic Schools* (Chelmsford: Matthew James, 2008).

Nouwen, H. J., *The Return of the Prodigal: A Story of Homecoming* (London: Darton, Longman & Todd, 1994).

O'Donohue, J., *Benedictus: A Book of Blessings* (London: Bantam Press, 2007).

O'Leary, D., *Begin with the Heart: Recovering a Sacramental Imagination* (Blackrock: Columba Press, 2008).

Palmer, S., *Toxic Childhood* (London: Orion, 2006).

Purnell, A. P. SJ, *Our Faith Story: An Education in Faith* (London: HarperCollins, 1985).

Radcliffe, T. OP, *What is the Point of Being a Christian?* (London: Burns & Oates, 2005).

Rohr, R. OFM, *Things Hidden: Scripture as Spirituality* (Cincinnati: St Anthony Messenger Press, 2008).

Rolheiser, R. OMI, *Prayer: Our Deepest Longing* (Cincinnati: Franciscan Media, 2013).

Schreck, A., *The Compact History of the Catholic Church* (Cincinnati: Servant Books, 2009).

Vanier, J., *Becoming Human* (London: Darton, Longman & Todd, 1999).

West-Burnham, J. & Jones, V.H., *Spiritual and Moral Development in Schools* (London: Network Continuum, 2007).